Jeff Schimmel's
MAXIMUM SCREENWRITING

25 COMMONLY ASKED QUESTIONS AND STRAIGHT ANSWERS

Jeff Schimmel

Gloriousarah Publishing

LOS ANGELES, CA

Copyright © 2017 by **Jeff Schimmel**

All rights reserved. No part of this publication may be reproduced, distributed, or transmitted in any form or by any means, including photocopying, recording, or other electronic or mechanical methods, without the prior written permission of the publisher, except in the case of brief quotations embodied in critical reviews and certain other noncommercial uses permitted by copyright law. For permission requests, write to the publisher, addressed "Attention: Permissions Coordinator," at the address below.

Jeff Schimmel
Gloriousarah Publishing
P.O. Box 1522
Agoura Hills, CA 91376
www.maximumscreenwriting.com

Publisher's Note: Although the author and publisher have made every effort to ensure that the information in this book was correct at press time, the author and publisher do not assume and hereby disclaim any liability to any party for any loss, damage, or disruption caused by errors or omissions, whether such errors or omissions result from negligence, accident, or any other cause.

Maximum Screenwriting / Jeff Schimmel. — 1st ed.
ISBN 978-0-9997390-0-6

Cover design, Book layout and production by Paul Dell, www.pauldell.com

Dedicated to my girls:

To my wife, Gloria. It's hard being a writer, but I'm sure it's even harder being married to one. Thank you for putting up with me.

To my daughter, Sarah. While I've loved everything my work as a writer has allowed us to do as a family, I've hated every minute away from you. T.I.S.V.S.B.A.D.A.A.D.

MY SINCEREST THANKS

Roxanne Ruane—You've helped me tremendously and tirelessly throughout the years, organizing my classes, sharing your humor, and most recently by triple-checking this book. In other words, if it doesn't turn out right, it's your fault. Just kidding. Or am I?

Colin (Last Name Classified)—For the awesome, ice cold Grey Goose, mediocre sushi, great conversation and friendship from afar.

Carlo Dall'Olmo and Phoenix Screenwriters Association—For graciously inviting me to speak to Arizona writers, time and time again, and keeping me connected to my adopted home town.

Dante Bacani and Chicago Screenwriters Network—For introducing me to the Windy City's vibrant writing community, but not the Bears or deep dish pizza. Yet.

To all the writers across the country who attend my weekend seminars, participate in my webinars and listen to my "Flip The Script" radio show—Your kindness and support are much appreciated.

Paul Dell—For suggesting this book, nagging me until I finally wrote it, designing it, putting it together, providing endless tech support, and sharing nearly 25 years of laughs mostly born of the absurdity inherent in show business. If people buy this book and enjoy it, I'll have to admit you were right. If they don't, please stop giving me suggestions.

Sandy Schimmel Gold—A source of love, encouragement and support, and someone who knows how glorious, and painful, artistic expression can be.

Bobby Schimmel—It all began the day I gave you a ride to Century City in the 1980s, which led to your request that I tell someone my idea for a movie. You introduced me to Mike Gardner who immediately introduced me to Gerry Abrams and Gerry Isenberg who quickly introduced me to Stu Miller who eventually introduced me to Jim Kellem who then gave me a random script to read that finally led me to Rodney Dangerfield and Harold Ramis.

Mom and Dad—Infinite thank yous—for just about everything.

TESTIMONIALS

"Jeff's clear ability to communicate his technique is responsible for my greater understanding of structure and character development. He is a generous artist with a vast knowledge of a difficult medium, limitless energy to teach, and writers at every level would do well to hear his approach."

PAUL JOHANSSON
Actor, Director, Producer, Emmy Award-winning Writer
One Tree Hill, Mad Men, Alpha Dog, Lonesome Dove, Beverly Hills 90210

"I've worked with great writer/producers, but few of Jeff's caliber. His grasp of structure, character, and comedy is superior. More important, he writes with a level of passion, style, and professionalism rarely seen in our business."

DAN ANGEL
Writer/Producer
The X Files, Young Blades

"Jeff Schimmel's work is always original and fresh. If he's willing to share his knowledge, you'd be smart to listen."

STAN LATHAN
Director/Producer
Hill Street Blues, Miami Vice, Falcon Crest, Roc

"If Jeff Schimmel's teaching, you're learning. He's a Director's writer/producer who leads with creativity, grace and humor."

KELLY HOMMON
Director/Producer
Real Time with Bill Maher, Beyond The Break, Mind of Mencia

"Of all the people I've worked with, Jeff is one of the very few who really knows how to tell a story, and how to successfully navigate a difficult industry. Everything Jeff teaches, he's lived—making him an invaluable resource."

PAUL DELL
Writer/Producer
The George Carlin Show, USA High, G.I. Joe

CONTENTS

Introduction 3
Original Characters 5
Superhero 11
Bad Outline 15
Notes From Strangers 27
Next Level Characters 31
Learning To Love The Rope 45
Script Title 49
Main Characters 51
Silly Things Writers Say 53
IMDB 57
Partners 61
Should I Have A Partner 65
Can I Sell A Script 71
The Use Of Profanity 75
Contests And Festivals 81
Script For The Money 93
Talking To Executives 97
Work For Free 101
Sell The Idea 107
Mentor 111
Script Length 117
Script Dos And Don'ts 121
Misc. 133
13 Commandments 141
How I Got Started 145
My Credits 161
Outlining 171
Defeating Procrastination 185
Story—The Rewrite 209
Story—Wild Pitch 215
Story—Buried Treasure 221

Jeff Schimmel's
MAXIMUM SCREENWRITING

INTRODUCTION

MAKE SURE YOU READ THIS

I'll keep it brief.

Although I've been a Writer/Producer in L.A. since the '80s, I never intended to write a book about screenwriting. Many already exist, most of them quite good and very helpful. But now, after spending seven years teaching my own curriculum in weekend seminars around the country, and noticing that many of the attendees have the same concerns from one city to the next, I decided to provide answers to some of the questions most often asked. The questions are real, asked by students at every level of experience and writing skill, and I've composed my written responses as if I were speaking directly to them. I never record my classes, so these answers are not merely transcripts. Hopefully reading these pages will be fun, informative and encouraging.

Don't get me wrong. By writing this book, I'm not saying that I have more or better knowledge or insights than other writers or teachers out there. Not at all. You can learn a tremendous amount from anyone who has gone before. What I've set out to do is give you my best advice and honest opinion on some of the issues I've encountered, and which you will likely run into when working as a writer.

I've included my simple strategy for defeating procrastination, as well as my method for creating a foolproof outline for your script. Without a doubt, these are two major problem areas writers everywhere seem to have in common, and the feedback I've received from my students and colleagues confirms that the techniques I provide really do work. But, you've got to do your part.

If you're looking for a manual that will tell you how to format the pages of a script, where to insert parentheticals when describing a character's attitude when delivering dialogue, or to explain the Three Act Structure upon which screenplays are built, this isn't the book for you. Maybe Volume #2 will include those topics, but I seriously doubt it. At least in L.A., you can close your eyes, throw a dart and hit one of those treatises. In the meantime, I'll let you in on a little secret. Formatting is already built into the Final Draft software program, and you can learn all about parentheticals and story structure, for free, on YouTube and countless websites.

If you read this book and walk away with at least one or two big pieces of valuable guidance that will help you avoid deadly mistakes and give you a better chance of succeeding as a screenwriter, then we'll both be happy.

Jeff Schimmel
www.maximumscreenwriting.com

QUESTION ONE

ORIGINAL CHARACTERS

What is the first step a writer should take when it comes to creating original characters?

I've never heard of there being a compulsory "first step" for creating characters, so enjoy the unfettered freedom of employing whatever method works best for you. I imagine that every writer approaches this task differently, and I would only caution you against the urge to cut corners. Be thorough. And when launching into the process, never lose sight of the fact that compelling original characters are mandatory in every script, regardless of genre, and without them, it will be impossible to construct a story worth telling.

If you don't already have a reliable procedure in place to help formulate characters, I can suggest a very simple method that I believe is extremely beneficial when it comes to assembling original characters from the ground up. It's a lot of work, but it's not hard work. Actually, it can be a lot of fun.

The strategy that I'm about to share with you will keep you on track, and if you stick with it, it will force you to fill in all the blanks about your characters at the earliest stage of writing before you even type FADE IN. Basically, you can choose to spend the time now or spend twice as much time later. I don't envy a writer who gets to a certain point in their screenplay only to realize that they don't know their characters well enough to predict what they will think or say, or how they will act in a given situation. Do you really want to stop down completely and figure it out at that time? Or do you want to resort to something even worse, which is to continue writing without the answers?

If you should decide to take my advice, begin by carefully considering every conceivable facet and nuance of the many people who will be living out their lives on your pages, and then spend the requisite amount of time to become better acquainted with these folks than anyone else in the world ever will be. They are essentially your children, so it is imperative that you know them as well as you know your own kids. If you don't have children, fake it.

Here goes. Real people are made up of an incredibly long list of component parts, and the best way to determine what makes any person the way they are, which will likely explain their actions, opinions, and choice of words, is to interview them. I prefer to interrogate them, which is a little more aggressive. Pretend they're a suspect, you're a detective, and give them the third degree. Put together a set of questions and then, as the writer, you have the responsibility to decide on the right answers. Remember, you're every character's parent. They get their DNA directly from you. Every characteristic they possess originates in your imagination. If you can't speak for them, then you haven't given their existence, and their absolute necessity to your story enough thought.

Before you begin the questioning, keep in mind that real people are attracted to real people, and can usually smell a phony. For example, when I'm reading a script or watching a movie, I find it hard to connect with a character when I can't fully understand their actions, motivations, emotions, frustrations, etc. While I may not like who they are, what they say, or what they do, if the writer clearly communicates everything I need to know about a character, chances are it will make sense to me and I will arrive at the intended conclusion.

This list contains the kinds of questions I would recommend you always ask your characters before you ever think of writing anything about them. If you can't settle on an answer, keep thinking about your story and what you need the individual characters to accomplish for you. Whatever you do, don't quit.

In no particular order:
- Character's name?
- Character's age?
- Where does the character live?
- Character's marital status? (Or other important relationships)
- Does the character have children or other significant familial relationships?
- Who does the character live with or spend most of their time with?
- Character's race/ethnicity?
- Character's sexual orientation?
- Character's social status?
- Character's highest level of education?
- Character's occupation?
- Character's relationship with superiors?
- Character's feelings about co-workers?
- How do co-workers feel about the character?
- Character's cultural aspects, including dietary restrictions, rivalries, gender roles, etc.?
- Character's religion, including astrology, atheism, belief in psychics, etc.?
- Who is the character's hero, even if it is an improved version of the character himself/herself?
- Character's life goals, hopes, dreams, etc.?
- What are the character's disappointments in life?

- Is the character socially skillful or awkward in public?
- Character's physical appearance?
- Character's feelings about his/her physical appearance?
- Character's mood on an average day?
- Does the character perceive himself/herself as a winner or loser?
- Character's outlook on life and his/her future?
- Character's best friend?
- Character's enemy?
- Character's relationship with close family members, both in present day and when growing up, including birth order?
- How does character perceive members of the opposite sex, how does this influence his/her behavior, and how is character perceived by members of the opposite sex?
- Character's political views?
- Character's heartbreaks?
- Character's fears?
- Character has resentment for which people or situations?
- Character's biggest secret(s)?
- Character's strengths?
- Character's weaknesses?
- Character's definition of personal success?
- Character's physical handicap?
- Character's habits, such as smoking, gambling, etc.?
- Character's speech patterns/impediments, such as accent, lisp, stuttering, etc.?

- Character's behavioral/psychological peculiarities, such as obsessive-compulsive disorder, hypochondriasis, anger, etc.?
- Character's biggest flaw(s)?
- Character's piercings, tattoos, mohawk haircut, etc.?
- Character's fashion/dress and personal grooming?
- Does character drive a car, ride a bike, take the bus, etc.?
- What kind of music does the character like/dislike?
- What kind of tv shows/movies does the character like/dislike?
- Character's favorite possession?
- Character's hobby or favorite past-time activity?
- Character's special talent?
- Where has the character always wanted to go?
- Character's like/dislike of personal pets or animals in general?
- Do any of these adjectives, or others, accurately describe character? Arrogant, passive, cocky, judgmental, flirtatious, crude, reckless, sentimental, logical, clueless, selfish, selfless, macho, cunning, materialistic, passionate, abusive, rebellious, vulgar, finicky, trusting, mellow, coldhearted, superstitious, etc.?

Now that you've compiled an in-depth profile of each prominent or vital character, it's time to ask the two questions that have always been the most meaningful to me. The answers will reveal even more and will get you thinking more deeply about your main characters.

- What is the defect or gaping "hole" that exists in the character's heart or existence in general?

- What will it take for that defect or "hole" to finally be healed, and for the character to finally feel complete?

Those two questions are meant to help you discover a figurative hole in a character's heart. Believe it or not, a writer in one of my weekend seminars blurted out that none of his main characters had, thank goodness, cardiac issues. I immediately called for a bathroom break so that I could go outside and punch myself in the face.

When it comes to the interview process, I wouldn't expect anyone to be able to answer every one of the questions listed above without giving them a lot of serious thought. I also know that many writers will resist the process and say that it isn't necessary to know all this stuff about anyone, whether in a script or even in real life. For example, why do I need to know how my main character feels about family members or whether or not they have spirituality or religion in their lives?

I understand that you may question this process. For example, your main character's specific religious beliefs may never come up in your script. You may never allude to their faith. But if he or she is committing an immoral act and are experiencing a guilty conscience as a result of what occurs when their actions and even minimal religious beliefs collide, that might reasonably manifest itself in their behavior and/or emotional output.

Try not to judge my interrogation method of character development too quickly or too harshly. Try it. I wouldn't suggest it if I didn't think you'd be very satisfied with the results.

QUESTION TWO

SUPERHERO

I've been working on a superhero script based on an original character I came up with in high school, but it's on hold right now. Even though there have been a ton of movies about Superman, Batman, Ironman and now Wonder Woman, a guest speaker told our writing group that it's a waste of time for us to write about our own superhero characters. Is she right?

I think she is. Yes, there have been a tremendous number of superhero movies over the last 40 years or so, dating back to Christopher Reeve in the first modern Superman film, and I'm pretty sure that most of them, if not every one of them, is based on a character from either Marvel Comics or DC Comics. If I had known when I was a kid that comic book superheroes would be such a big deal, I probably would have paid more attention to them and bought some collectibles that I could put up for auction on eBay. I must admit that the only superhero film I've seen since the 1970s is "Ironman" with Robert Downey, Jr. As you already know, superheroes give the studios the huge, summer blockbusters they count on to keep some of them from filing for Chapter 11 bankruptcy protection, and it seems like they'll be cranking those suckers out forever.

What the guest speaker may have been trying to tell you, perhaps a little too bluntly, was that movie studios aren't interested in buying superhero projects that don't have a proven appeal or track record of any kind. Batman might not be everyone's cup of tea, but the comic books have been on the radar forever, movies featuring that character seem to work, and if the story is good and the cast is good, they aren't really taking much of a risk. If done well and if it captures the authentic vibe of the particular superhero, the odds are the film will score with the comic book crowd, plus the rest of the folks who like big, noisy action.

If you come up with a superhero of your own, who knows about it except you? Who's a fan? Nobody, except maybe your friends, family or the girl from school or work who won't go out with you because the whole comic book thing has her convinced that you're an incurable nerd. I'm not judging, but she probably is. Is there a built-in audience for your original character? No. It will take a lot of time and money to convince people to give your superhero a try. They will have to feel like it's worth the price of a ticket to find out if he's awesome or lame. That's why Marvel and DC are the go-to folks for that type of film. The studios continue to bet on what has worked before, but if you're a lover of the genre, then you know that there have also been some major league duds along the way. Yet another reason why it isn't prudent for studios to invest a fortune in an untried main character in the superhero genre. If the studio bosses can avoid a disaster, they will. I don't know what else I can say other than conventional wisdom dictates that the industry is averse to losing money, and if you approach them with a new superhero, you represent anything but a sure thing to them.

Here's a suggestion that you might not hate, even though it's almost certainly not what you want to hear. When you have the time and enthusiasm, finish your superhero screenplay and sit on it for a while. If you have confidence in yourself and you're able to write some great stuff, get an agent, make a sale, maybe pick up a studio script assignment or two, your unseen, original superhero screenplay can always resurface later, once you have some force behind your name and a winning track record. If people love your work, they might be willing to take a chance on your project. Might.

So, my advice differs from your guest speaker in this respect: Don't quit. Impossible might be harsh, and it might just be temporary. If you love it, finish it and put it away until you're so damn good, no one can say no to you.

QUESTION THREE

BAD OUTLINE

I'm about to start writing an action movie, and I want to be sure I've outlined it properly. How will I know when I have enough?

I could tell, as soon as he used the word "enough," that he hadn't finished outlining, but was hoping I would say he had. Was he really just trying to generate "enough" of an outline to begin writing? If so, he's missing the point of having a truly well-developed outline. I made him an offer he didn't refuse—which was for him to show me what he already had during the seminar's lunch break, if he felt confident about it, and I'd give him my honest opinion. Fair enough?

The student met with me, and as he chowed down on a #13 sub from Jersey Mike's, I read his outline. It was so short, he only took about two bites before I was ready to discuss his work, or more accurately, the lack thereof. Within minutes, he seemed too nauseous to continue eating, but I considered that to be a good sign. He had seen the error of his ways. He listened intently, asked a few questions, nodded a lot, took some notes, and by the time lunch was over, he agreed to let me share his brief outline with the class that was about to reconvene. In exchange for this real-life ammunition, which would be highly illustrative to his classmates, I invited him to meet me that evening for a story consultation. Free of charge.

Below is his actual screenplay outline, the version he hoped was enough:

ACTION MOVIE OUTLINE (ORIGINAL DRAFT)

- Bank robbery takes place. School Teacher was there. Didn't see the bad guys well enough to identify them.

- Bad Guys are worried about getting caught. Bad Guy #1 remembers there was someone outside the bank that might have seen them. They need to find out who he is.

- School Teacher picks up his dinner date. While driving to their destination, the Bad Guys arrive and chase them. School Teacher and the Woman get away safely.

- School Teacher and the Woman have dinner, then make love.

- The next day, School Teacher finds out his date has gone missing. Police don't know what happened, but a note from the Bad Guys says they will kill the Woman unless School Teacher gives himself up.

- School Teacher looks for clues. He doesn't know who Bad Guys are and is worried.

- School Teacher gets drunk and angry. He takes his weapons and decides to go after Bad Guys.

END ACT ONE

That's it, folks. You just read his entire outline. One painfully apparent problem was that he was satisfied with only outlining Act One. The other problem, and I hope you noticed it as well, is that his outline was beyond minimal, and I will say he left out more information than he included. Could the writer, a very nice, well-intentioned young man, use an outline this incomplete as his guide to a solid, 110-page screenplay? I don't see how, unless his preferred method of writing includes spending long periods of time sitting at his computer, thinking about what he needs to fill up the holes in the story and the blank spaces on the page—a clear path to doom.

That night, despite having spent about 10 hours on my feet teaching a seminar and losing my voice, I followed through on my promise and met the writer for a drink. I expected some push back on the notes I gave earlier that day, but I was happy to hear that the writer had already given his deficient outline some additional thought and he was ready, willing and able to talk to me about what was missing. Over the course of the next two hours, we threw a bunch of ideas around, compared thinly drawn characters to more developed incarnations, spoke about stories and scenes from some of our favorite movies, etc. It was fun, and far more productive than either of us expected it to be.

I always feel a strong sense of satisfaction when I'm able to demonstrate, especially to a new writer, that working through an outline doesn't have to feel like a punishment. After all, you're about to invest a tremendous amount of time and talent into a story that you allegedly love. Don't you want to get to know it better?

Over the next few days, the writer typed up his new and improved outline, and it definitely had taken several steps in the right direction. It wasn't, by any means, perfect, nor would the writer stop adding more details to his outline just because he made significant progress. He would continue to think it through and fill in the blanks. Using my method of outlining shown in my class, the story remained organized. He could see where he needed more story, and even though the amount of vital information continued to increase, sticking to what he learned about my way of doing things, he was able to plug each piece of new material into its proper slot.

What you are about to see is not his final outline. But this should give you a pretty good idea of how much more complete the writer's outline turned out to be after a few hours of work that he didn't expect to be so pleasurable. If all he got from my class was the knowledge that outlining can be more fun, and less of a drag, then he got his money's worth.

Look at his new and improved outline and ask yourself how much more helpful it would be as a writing tool.

ACTION MOVIE OUTLINE (NEW DRAFT)

BEGINNING OF ACT ONE

SETTING: PHOENIX, ARIZONA—1973

MAIN CHARACTER: CASEY STONE. Late 30's. High School Science Teacher and varsity soccer team coach. Ex-Army Ranger. Still in great physical condition. Looks ten years younger than he is. Friends teasingly call him "Sunshine" because he used to blast KC & the Sunshine Band in his Humvee in Iraq.

Casey's life is routine, borders on boring. His schedule is reminiscent of military regimentation. It's mostly teaching, coaching, and alone time. He very rarely ventures out for recreation, keeps to himself, and it seems likely that he is hiding something that still haunts him from his days in the Army. His behavior is a little strange considering he's someone who lived on the edge but who now doesn't seem willing to take too many risks.

Casey is at an ATM outside when a local bank is robbed. He completes his transaction and throws his receipt in the trash. While other people are diving for cover clearly afraid, Casey is as cool as a cucumber. The BAD GUYS get away in a black SUV before the Police arrive. While Casey is something of a hermit, his military experience has conditioned him for high-stress situations. When others are afraid, Casey excels. During the bank robbery with shots fired, Casey's blood pressure doesn't go up at all.

The POLICE speak to potential WITNESS at the scene, but they let Casey go almost immediately because he says he didn't see anything other than the black SUV as it left. He didn't catch the license plate, and the Bad Guys were wearing masks. Casey really doesn't want to get involved.

Later, Casey is at the gym doing his customary workout. He watches the news on TVs suspended above the equipment. There's a report about the bank robbery. The Police have no clues yet.

In a warehouse, the Bad Guys count the money they stole from the bank. They argue disappointedly because it isn't as much as they thought they would get. One of the Bad Guys, the youngest and most innocent one, is afraid that they will be caught. He panics and only calms down when he is comforted by one of the other Bad Guys who might be related to him. Perhaps he is an older brother? The two other Bad Guys talk as if they have lengthy criminal records and have been arrested and jailed for this type of thing in the past. If they are caught, they will go back to prison for a long time, and the RINGLEADER isn't about to let that happen.

The Ringleader sends his EXPERIENCED PARTNER back to the bank in a regular car to retrieve something from the garbage can by the ATM machine. The Ringleader saw a guy, most likely Casey, doing an ATM transaction as the Bad Guys hopped into the black SUV, and he wants to know who that person is because he might be a witness to their crime. The Ringleader says there are ways to trace the receipt account information back to the person at the ATM and they will be able to ascertain Casey's identity. These days, the more high-tech crime of identity theft is common, and it won't be hard to get the information, especially since the Ringleader knows a hacker he can pay to obtain the information.

Casey's love interest: LULU, early 40's. She's a hottie, especially for her age, but it's clear she isn't the kind of girl you'd want to bring home to meet Mama, unless Mama is a retired prostitute. From the way she dresses and speaks, Lulu might be a stripper, exotic dancer, escort, etc. Casey doesn't know too much about Lulu, but he isn't really interested in a serious relationship so he keeps things on a very shallow level. At best, this is simple companionship with some physical benefits. Casey is withdrawn when it comes to genuine intimacy. Lulu isn't necessarily his type but she provides comfort to him, and

Casey is known to be vulnerable to people in need of help. Maybe all Lulu needs is a kind word.

Casey leaves the gym and goes home. He lives in the kind of older rental house that a teacher can afford. Nothing fancy inside. Casey dresses up nicely, puts on some cologne, checks himself in the mirror, and leaves. It must be something out of the ordinary because Casey isn't usually concerned with his appearance to this extent. He drives off in his sporty, but kind of beat up car. This might be a special night.

Casey arrives at Lulu's apartment. It's obvious that she isn't making much money. Probably just scraping by. Casey picks her up for what looks like a date. She's wearing an outfit that is probably her most conservative but is still very revealing.

Two of the Bad Guys, absent the Ringleader, have been following Casey but he was unaware of that. Casey and Lulu make small talk. She is happy to be out with him, and he tries to relax and have fun, but it isn't easy. When he's home alone, on most nights he doesn't have to engage anyone with small talk. The Bad Guys pull up alongside Casey at a red light. The younger Bad Guy points a gun shakily at Casey. Casey floors it and takes evasive action to escape.

Bad ass car chase. Casey is an excellent driver and can take tight turns, control skids, etc. He has no fear of high speeds, but he is scaring the hell out of Lulu who wonders what it's all about. Who are these guys? Casey doesn't know. Lots of high energy and near misses, and Casey eventually loses the Bad Guys with a slick J-turn maneuver at a break in the median. Once again, the quiet, unassuming dude is a monster in a pinch.

Lulu is shaken, but Casey doesn't have an elevated pulse. He's been through a lot worse. He doesn't know those men or their car or why they pointed a gun, and he believes it might have been a case of mistaken identity. Casey tells Lulu not to worry, and since he promised her a nice dinner, he doesn't think they should miss out on it. They go to the restaurant.

Casey and Lulu have dinner, a fancier meal than either of them has had in a long time. They joke about how it was almost a disaster and are happy that they went through with the date. They are both in need of a decent friend they can be genuine with and sadly, they appear to be alone in the world. Casey is probably the most upstanding guy Lulu ever went out with, and Lulu is probably the only girl, of any kind, that Casey has gone out with in years.

After dinner, Casey and Lulu walk hand in hand to Casey's car in the parking lot. When Casey wants to open the door for Lulu, behaving like a true gentleman, she guides his hand to open the door to the back seat instead. This is very unexpected, but not necessarily unwanted. Uncomfortable, Casey hesitates, but Lulu kisses him and opens the door herself. She has made this decision, and he shouldn't fear that he is taking advantage of her. She gets into the back seat of the car and pulls Casey in beside her. It's been a long time since Casey had this kind of interaction with a woman, and it shows. Lulu seems to really care about him, and she wants him to know it.

The next morning, Casey has a little more spring in his step. He is getting dressed to go to work, and when he goes into the closet to pick out a shirt, he stands on top of a big, green footlocker to grab a sweater from the shelf. When he steps down, he looks at the footlocker. It is olive drab, painted with white stenciled letters that spell out his name, his serial number, etc. It's a relic from this days in the military and is padlocked.

Casey is in class teaching. The students are very attentive. He is enthusiastic as he speaks, and they like and respect him. A girl comes in and tells Casey that he's wanted in the Principal's office. It seems urgent.

Casey enters the front office where the PRINCIPAL and DETECTIVE LIEUTENANT HARRISON are waiting for him. Bad news. Lulu was abducted from her apartment. Her neighbors reported a ruckus. Whoever kidnapped Lulu left a bizarre note. Casey reads it. To his surprise, it says that the Bad Guys are willing to let Lulu go, but only as a trade for Casey. Strange. No one, including Casey, understands what's happening but Casey tells Detective Harrison about the car chase from the night before. This is extremely sensitive, and a woman's life is at stake. The Bad Guys threaten that they will kill Lulu if Casey doesn't agree to their terms.

Detective Harrison is stumped. How are these unknown people and seemingly unrelated events connected? The bank robbery doesn't even come up in their discussion because it doesn't appear to be relevant. Whatever skeletons Lulu has in her closet are also unknown. She might have a checkered past, but she protects those details. Casey thinks it through and convinces Detective Harrison that, whoever the Bad Guys are, they are after Casey and not Lulu. Otherwise, why would they want to trade for Casey? If true, that would mean someone has it in for Casey, but for what reason? Does it date back to his time in the Army? That doesn't make sense, because of how long it's been.

At the Bad Guy Warehouse, the Ringleader is slapping Lulu around. The youngest Bad Guy isn't in favor of this and tries to object, but what can he do? Lulu is confused. She really doesn't know what they want Casey for, and if they know who he is, then they must know where they can find him. The Ringleader informs Lulu that if Casey doesn't agree to the trade, she will be killed. They're not messing around.

Casey leaves the school and drives to his friend Jerry's house. JERRY SANDERS was with Casey in Iraq. They have been buddies ever since. If there is anyone Casey can trust, it's Jerry.

Casey explains what happened. Jerry doesn't have any theories that make sense. He does, however, agree that it all must be about Casey, not Lulu. She is just a bargaining chip. Jerry has Casey retrace his steps and without giving it much thought, Casey talks about the bank robbery that occurred earlier the day before. Could they be related? Casey doesn't know how. He didn't really know anything of importance and told that to the police. He purposefully stayed out of the situation.

Jerry pleads with Casey to let the police handle this situation. Jerry mentions a girl named Loreen, and this elicits a major reaction from Casey. It seems to hurt him deep inside. Casey storms out and Jerry instantly regrets saying anything about Loreen. It's clear something about her name has triggered Casey's demons.

Casey goes to Lulu's apartment. The front door is sealed with a Police Department order and Crime Scene tape. Casey goes around to the back of the building, climbs up to Lulu's balcony, and opens her window. He enters and begins to search Lulu's apartment for a clue, but what kind? Is there something in her place that would lead the Bad Guys, whoever they are, to Casey? He tries, but no luck.

Casey returns home. It's night. A police car is parked in his driveway. Detective Harrison has been trying to locate Casey. Concerned for Casey's safety, they posted a guard at his house. Now that Casey is home, he asks the Police Officers to leave. He doesn't think he needs their protection. They drive off.

Casey is very upset. Inside his house, he has a beer or two, and paces while trying to figure out this situation. He sits down on his couch and looks at the large scrapbook that is part of a stack of books on his coffee table. It has a photo of a pretty woman on the cover. Once Casey sees it, whatever is in that album is clearly emotional dynamite for Casey. He looks inside and swallows hard when he sees a mountain of old, yellowing newspaper clippings from Military newspapers, and they are all about the abduction of a female U.S. Army soldier in Iraq. Terrorists grabbed her, and apparently, Casey was involved with her and her rescue mission. The clippings feature photos of the same pretty woman, LOREEN STROMAN, along with headlines that say things about her kidnapping and give updates on the Army's efforts to find and free her. There is a headline that recounts, in detail, a botched rescue attempt and a grisly death for the pretty woman. This article knocks the wind out of Casey.

Casey throws his beer bottle against the wall. He was part of the team that tried to rescue Loreen. He agonizes about that situation and the current, similar predicament with Lulu. He screams that he can't risk it again. The last time a woman he cared about was taken hostage, he tried his best but was unable to rescue her. He blames himself for her death, believing that he did something wrong while trying to save her. He's convinced it was his fault she is dead. Casey sees his own reflection in a window and yells at himself. Somehow, it has happened again. Someone close to him is in trouble and this time he doesn't want to mess it up and get her killed. He has been given a second chance in life to fix things. This mission cannot fail.

A little tipsy, but motivated and capable, Casey goes to his closet and pulls out the green footlocker. He unlocks and opens it to reveal an arsenal of weapons. He has a few semi-automatic assault rifles, handguns, knives, ammunition, etc. Seeing these items bring back unspoken memories. He selects his favorite sidearm, a Beretta 9mm, and a box of shells.

Before leaving his house, Casey peeks outside to make sure no one is waiting to ambush him. The coast seems clear, but he still chooses to sneak out the side door into the darkness. Casey is dressed in black, and his face is obscured by black camouflage paint. He looks like Rambo, in fatigues.

Casey gets in his car. Before driving off, he calls Detective Harrison. He tells him that he's given it some thought and he will just handle this situation himself. He is the only person he trusts to get this done right, without getting Lulu killed. Detective Harrison, knowing nothing about Casey or his past, doesn't understand. He tells Casey to stay home and wait to hear from him, but Casey refuses. He's determined. The Police have their schedule, and Casey has his. To avoid being tracked by GPS, Casey turns and tosses his phone into the bushes outside his house. This is it. Things will be different this time. The Bad Guys don't know it, but whoever took Lulu is as good as dead. You've messed with the very dangerous Casey Stone, and he's about to be all up in their shit!

END OF ACT ONE

Okay, fellow writers. Like I said before, this outline isn't perfect or complete, but I think you'll agree it's a lot further along than the Swiss cheese outline we saw a few days before. Is this the final version? Probably not. Will the writer keep coming up with cool ideas for story beats, action scenes, and character traits? Before he sits down to write, will he continue filling in blanks, making changes, and adding more complications? I sure hope so.

The point of this exercise was to prove to this writer, and the rest of the students in my class, that you don't know "enough" to start writing your screenplay until you absolutely, positively know as much as you can possibly know. That's the best time to type FADE IN.

QUESTION FOUR

NOTES FROM STRANGERS

Almost everyone who reads my script thinks it's really good, but one or two people had some suggestions on how I could make it even better. I don't want to make the mistake of taking their word for it, so how do I know who or what to believe?

I know this might sound silly, but if I were you, I wouldn't give very much credence to the notes given by anyone who hasn't already written more scripts than you have at this stage of your career—and done them correctly. Some of the most dangerous opinions you will encounter come from the totally uninitiated, yet well-intentioned, people in your life, such as friends and family members. You're much safer taking advice or direction from an established screenwriter, professional reader, development executive, legitimate producer, or writing instructor at a reputable school.

Look at it this way. When you were in nursery school, and you brought home your first finger painting, what did your Mom do? Most likely she hugged you and kissed you, called you an artistic genius and then proudly displayed that mess on the refrigerator door for all to see and admire. It didn't matter to your Mom what the picture looked like; she was going to love it unconditionally because she loved you unconditionally. The same goes for your script, except a finger painting only takes a few minutes to create, while a writer can easily spend a year or more agonizing over a screenplay. The last thing you need is a casual assessment from someone who has likely never even seen a script before.

You can survive criticism of your finger painting. But you're all grown up now, and you've decided to pursue screenwriting. Even if your Mom doesn't want you to be a writer because it isn't the easiest career to get off the ground or the most stable, if you give her a script to read, she probably isn't going to say anything to hurt your feelings. The same goes for other family members, spouses, significant others, friends, etc. The odds are, people who care about you and who wish the best for you will tend to reward your hard work by telling you that your screenplay is destined to win an Oscar. The folks who are always there to support your endeavors will place their stamp of approval on anything your write. I mean, what would you expect them to say? Then again, if you pressed them for a couple of cogent notes on your story, could your friends or family members provide reliable guidance? I don't know the people you hang out with, but if they're anything like my Mom and Dad, they either don't know what goes into the screenwriting process, or they can't comprehend why anyone in their right mind would want to spend their time reading or discussing what happens in a script or even analyze a movie playing at the neighborhood theater. When I showed my parents my first screenplay, they wanted to know why I gave up the practice of law for such foolishness. When I invited them to the taping of an episode I wrote for a hit sitcom, and told them the all-in cost was around $1,000,000 for that week of production, my Dad shook his head and said, "What a waste of money." I loved them dearly, but that's why I never asked them for suggestions.

My opinion, based on years of experience, is that one of the most perilous things a writer can do is to take advice from a stranger they met in a Meetup group, or another new writer who just happens to be occupying a nearby comfy chair at their local coffee shop. Is it really that easy to trust someone you just met who doesn't have any more insight into screenwriting than you do? I've met many writers who came up with solid, original stories, read books on screenwriting, honed their skills on preliminary drafts of a few scripts, and then devoted all their free time to crafting a screenplay they felt confident about, only to see it all go up in smoke because someone without any skin in the game gave them notes on how to fix what was wrong with their script—and they actually listened!

Many writers will be embarrassed right about now because I've accurately described a situation they've found themselves in recently. It happens far too frequently to be an accident. Wanting a script to be as good as it can be will lead some new writers to seek answers or approval from people with good intentions, but who have no idea what the heck they're talking about when it comes to building a story or writing a screenplay. You're looking for validation, probably from just about anyone, and you don't care where it comes from or how much trouble a kind word or two might end up causing you.

A nightmare scenario I've seen played out on several occasions over the years is one where a novice writer completes a screenplay, receives notes from someone ill-equipped to offer them, and the writer who strives to put his best foot forward then performs a total rewrite over a period of a few months, utilizing a road map some knucklehead dreamed up in about five minutes based on zero experience. It's hard enough to write a good script under the best of conditions, so I can't understand how anyone could think their script will somehow be improved by incorporating suggestions from an unqualified source.

Don't get me wrong. I'm not against writers' groups in general. If you can learn from guest lecturers or seasoned veterans in the industry who are willing to teach beginners, that's a rare and wonderful thing. You should definitely take advantage of those opportunities. If having friends in the group helps you to establish and enforce deadlines, and gives you a shoulder to cry on, that's even better. I would just caution against getting sucked into a "blind leading the blind" trap, where people who don't know what they're doing are teaching other people who don't know what they're doing, and where beginners are analyzing the scripts written by other beginners. If that's the case, be extremely careful.

It isn't impossible to have your script read by a professional, so why settle for an amateur? When I want an accurate diagnosis regarding a health issue, I consult a doctor, not a gardener. And I have an awesome gardener.

QUESTION FIVE

NEXT LEVEL CHARACTERS

Do you have suggestions on how we can give more unique dimensions to our characters, other than just knowing their physical description, likes, dislikes, habits, past experiences, etc.? For example, I feel like if I'm writing a screenplay where my main character has an occupation we've seen many times before, they might unintentionally be derivative, at least at the start.

There's a quick, fun exercise I enjoy using when I'm thinking about my characters, especially my main characters. I use this game when I'm trying to figure out why they're in the situation they're in, why they behave the way they do, how they're perceived by others who come into contact with them, what consequences they might face as a result of their conduct, etc. Obviously, I'd suggest that other writers try this approach, but definitely do so before you begin writing. That's the optimal time to explore your characters, and this tool will likely lead to story beats you never thought of before, which is a bonus. Again, I do a lot of thinking before I ever type FADE IN, and I implore you to do the same.

The easiest way for me to explain this process is to say that, when considering your main character, you keep going one step beyond what you already know about them. It can be a positive or a negative trait, behavior or action, but whichever way you go, it should have some type of meaningful impact on who they are. When you can take the character in question to another level of complexity, and then the next and the next, take a moment to recognize the increased value of what you have done, and then take the character to still another level. In the words of the late, great Michael Jackson, don't stop 'til you get enough.

All of us have a lot of stuff going on at the surface, things that are easy for others to see. Those characteristics help to inform our behavior and emotions. The more you can add, within reason, and as long as it continues to make sense for a specific character, the deeper you can dive into what makes the character tick, and the greater your understanding of them will be.

We all have secrets, idiosyncrasies, and things we generally aren't very proud of. We have strong points, but you need only look at the flip side to find our faults. We are worthy of praise and admiration for some things, hopefully, but are also ashamed of things we've done and for which we feel we are deserving of scorn. Nobody's perfect.

Your main character needs to grow across the arc of your story and if you've made this character a shining example of humanity without some significant defects, you need to blow them up, rethink the formula of who they really are, give their DNA a good scramble, and put the new and improved version of this character together so they can live inside the world of your story and make choices that match who they are and who you need them to be.

Someone who starts out being awesome in just about every way, and ends up being slightly more awesome at the end of your story, isn't worth rooting for, at least in my opinion. I tend to cheer for the underdog in almost every situation because they are usually overpowered by an adversary who seems to have limitless energy and resources. The good guy who is handsome, strong, powerful, popular, and has everything going their way, doesn't need my help or anyone else's. I can't imagine them ever struggling as they seek to overcome and achieve their goal. If a character is too perfect and things are too easy for her, I don't feel compelled to cross my fingers and pray for her to succeed. On the other hand, a flawed person who is willing to accept her shortcomings, and fights tooth and nail to correct her defects, is someone I'm more inspired to follow.

I will predict, right now, that some people are going to laugh when I say I want to use Mr. Miyagi from "The Karate Kid" movies as an example of this principle and process. The reason I've selected Mr. Miyagi is that it's so damn easy to understand how taking his character to another level or two made him a more meaningful mentor to Daniel La Russo.

What did we know about Mr. Miyagi right from the start? He's Asian. He's in charge of maintenance for the apartment complex in Reseda where Daniel and his mother live. When Daniel is attacked, we find out that Mr. Miyagi is skilled in martial arts of some kind. He soon takes a liking to young Daniel, and if we watched those movies on the most superficial level and didn't come to learn anything more about Mr. Miyagi, his character could merely, but admirably, fulfill his role as Daniel's karate teacher. Isn't that correct?

But to really get a feel for Mr. Miyagi, it was essential that the writer, Robert Mark Kamen, do exactly what I suggested all of you do, which is to figure out what else is true about Mr. Miyagi and to take him a step further, so that his actions, emotions, and goals make total sense, and deliver a deeper and much more satisfying result.

If you pay close attention while watching the first installment of "The Karate Kid," you will learn the following facts:

- Mr. Miyagi was originally from Okinawa.
- His father was a fisherman who taught Mr. Miyagi a form of karate that was passed down from father to son.
- Mr. Miyagi came to America at some point and was later taken to the Manzanar internment camp in California at the outset of World War II.
- He joined the U.S. Army and fought in Europe.
- He was wounded in combat and received a Purple Heart medal.

- Mr. Miyagi was part of the 442nd Regimental Combat Team, which was among the most decorated units in the war.
- He earned multiple medals for bravery, including the Congressional Medal of Honor. To have won our nation's highest honor, Mr. Miyagi would have had to kill enemy soldiers and risk his own life in some heroic way, while also saving his comrades from death.
- Mr. Miyagi had a wife who died during childbirth, along with their newborn son. This happened in Manzanar internment camp while he was serving overseas.

Like I said earlier, in order for Mr. Miyagi to fulfill his most basic role in "The Karate Kid," he only needed to teach Daniel how to fight. Was it absolutely necessary for you to know all of the other, seemingly irrelevant, details about Mr. Miyagi for him to be effective as Daniel's mentor? No. So, why did Robert Mark Kamen create a backstory like this for Mr. Miyagi? To me, it's simple but crucial.

Mr. Miyagi was living alone, with no family of his own. Mentoring Daniel, and allowing him to get close as their teacher-student relationship grew, gave Mr. Miyagi someone to take care of and be concerned about, and it also meant that Daniel would grow fond of Mr. Miyagi and care about him too. Mr. Miyagi lost his newborn son, before he could ever hold him, and he never got over it. We can all sympathize with that.

Mr. Miyagi suffers from tremendous guilt, for a variety of reasons. Killing people in a war, even enemy combatants takes a toll. Plus, surviving the war while his wife and child do not, envelops Mr. Miyagi in the kind of devastating guilt most of us could never imagine or hope to deal with. In some way, Mr. Miyagi could treat Daniel like a son and pass his knowledge of karate down to Daniel, the same way his father passed it on to Mr. Miyagi when he was a boy. Keep the chain unbroken.

You can tell from the medals Mr. Miyagi was awarded that he wasn't just a brave soldier, but was also exceptionally honorable. A man like Mr. Miyagi believes in fair play, and will not stand by and allow an innocent boy like Daniel to be bullied and ganged up on, nor will he allow Daniel to be targeted by a sinister, unprincipled man who purports to be an upstanding martial arts instructor. Mr. Miyagi will expose himself to the risk of harm to protect Daniel and will be a father figure to Daniel who has no real father in his life.

Mr. Miyagi promises to teach Daniel karate, but in exchange asks him to paint his fence, sand his floor, and wax his cars. This is most likely a glimpse into how Mr. Miyagi's father taught him karate in Okinawa, which we come to understand is a much deeper and more meaningful transaction than just giving a boy karate lessons for an hour a day in exchange for some small fee.

Mr. Miyagi gives Daniel a car as a gift, which is something more appropriate for a father to do. I've lived in several apartments over the years and was friendly with the handymen, gardeners, and landlords, but none of them ever gave me a car. At most, they said hello and did their job. It is understood, from Mr. Miyagi's warm behavior, that he and Daniel have begun to develop the kind of relationship which is invaluable and comforting to both.

When Daniel wins the tournament in the finale, the pride on Mr. Miyagi's face serves as the freeze frame which ends the movie. A karate teacher would undoubtedly be proud of his student for winning, but Daniel is more than Mr. Miyagi's student. The look on Mr. Miyagi's face says, "That's my boy!"

Think about it for a second. Throughout the majority of the film, Mr. Miyagi is a funny, happy go lucky guy. He is always teasing Daniel, and his dialogue is humorous. He is old school Japanese and spouts Eastern philosophy, but you can never quite be sure if he's serious or pulling Daniel's leg. But then, there's the scene when Daniel comes by at night to find Mr. Miyagi laid out, drunk off his ass, wearing his old World War II uniform with a box of his medals and a picture of his deceased wife next to him. Why is this cuddly prankster inebriated, mumbling sadly, and wearing this outfit? It's because he's a permanently tortured soul. Having Daniel in his life is as close as Mr. Miyagi has come to finding a magic ingredient to heal the gaping hole in his heart. What Daniel doesn't know is that Mr. Miyagi needs him infinitely more than Daniel needs to learn how to defend himself from bullies. This is why all of that information about Mr. Miyagi's character is so vital to the story. Without it, he's an amusing little clown who teaches a kid how to punch and kick. Mr. Miyagi is lonely and guilt-ridden, but through his emotional connection with Daniel, he has a chance to redeem himself, and save them both.

I would guess that while most people feel that Mr. Miyagi is a kind and generous man, they never really considered all the factors I just mentioned. Those factors make a big difference in telling a story and the process for making sure your characters have this kind of depth is at your fingertips. It's what I'm explaining now. If your main characters don't have these kinds of pluses and minuses swirling around beneath the surface, how compelling, and how authentically human, can they be?

When drilling down into your characters, it's helpful to play the "What If" game. Think about your character and then ask yourself "what if" a certain thing happened to him or her? Ask yourself what's worse than that, and keep going. One of the generic examples I often use in my class is a Priest who is suspected of molesting a child. I know it's an upsetting subject, but it is something terribly unfortunate that occurs in real life, and in films. The discomfort associated with this subject is part of the reason I like to use it for this exercise.

If a Priest has committed a sex crime against a child, it tells me something beyond disturbing about them. But then I think about what else lurks in the background of this Priest. What's worse than a local Priest who molested a child? A Priest who is also accused of perpetrating the same despicable crimes in another diocese, which caused him to be transferred to his current post.

Taking another step, can you think of something that complicates and worsens this already ghastly situation? What if the Bishop in the previous diocese sent the sex offender Priest to his new church assignment while having specific knowledge of his crimes, and only did so in an attempt to pass a hot potato? Committing these acts against children is an abomination, so how much worse is it that this Priest got away with it because those in charge knowingly swept his wrongdoings under the rug? Then, as follows logically, I would ask whether the Priest's past was divulged to the Bishop who presides over the new diocese. If so, even more people are aware of the Priest's bad acts and allow him to continue in his role as spiritual leader of a community.

It's been said that those who persecute people were once persecuted themselves. We can push this exercise a bit further by asking if this Priest was also molested when he was a child, perhaps as an altar boy, which might add another layer of pain to his state of mind. If I want to go to the extreme, I can delve still deeper by asking if this Priest could have committed an intentional and deadly act of violence against his own molester causing his death, and was never discovered as the assailant, or if the Priest may have accidentally killed one of the children he assaulted. I know, it's vile and disgusting. But if you're writing about this type of crime, or something along the lines of "Silence of the Lambs," you won't be able to adequately explore the horrors of what happens in real life if you can't go there when constructing your story. It's one reason I stick almost exclusively to comedy!

I'll give you another much shorter, and much lighter example of how a piece of information that seems inconsequential when you first learn of it becomes important to really understanding the actions of a character later in the story. It is admittedly silly, but it clearly illustrates the benefit you derive from something this insignificant and uncomplicated.

If you've seen "The Hangover," you probably remember the Ed Helms character, Stuart Price, the dentist who married a very sweet and down to earth stripper named Jade while severely under the influence during a Bachelor Party weekend in Las Vegas.

Stu is a nice guy, far from being a Casanova, which is why it makes sense that he tolerates an awful relationship with Melissa, a very unpleasant and incredibly overbearing girlfriend. If he didn't have Melissa, the odds are Stu might not have anyone. Melissa demands to know where Stu is going, what he's doing, and lets him know, in no uncertain terms, that she is the boss. He really can't refuse to answer, because he knows he can't win an argument with her. Stu is so afraid of Melissa that when she asks where the Bachelor Party is, he lies and tells her it's in Napa Valley. Stu knows that Melissa would never let him go to Las Vegas, and she even tells him that he had better not go to a strip club while he's away. Phil, one of the other guys on the trip, tells their mutual friends that Melissa has beaten Stu up in the past. It isn't out of the question.

The missing piece of the puzzle is that Melissa had sex with a bartender on a cruise ship, while she and Stu were already in a relationship. Stu knows about it and he is forced to accept it, because Melissa says so. Live with it, Stu, or good luck finding another girlfriend. Unlike Stu, Melissa can apparently do whatever she wants and Stu just has to take it. Imagine being in a relationship with someone who completely controls you, but who you cannot even question.

This turns out to be an important fact because when Stu marries Jade, an extremely nice girl, while in Las Vegas, he can't understand how it could have happened—even on a wild and crazy weekend like this one. Stu wonders how a nerdy weakling can get a girl as lovely as Jade? Yes, she's a stripper, but she's also a single mom with a soft heart and she's flattered that Stu, a professional man, even likes her. Wow, what a big departure for Stu who is totally unappreciated, manipulated and terrorized by Melissa.

When Stu realizes what he's done in Las Vegas, he is fearful of what Melissa will do when she finds out. Melissa, on the other hand, probably didn't give a rat's ass about Stu's feelings when she had sex with the bartender on a cruise ship, or when he found out about it. Jade gives Stu the affection, power, and self-confidence he so desperately needs to finally stand up for himself. Back in Los Angeles, Stu is a changed man and breaks it off with Melissa at his friend's wedding, shouting the reasons in front of the guests. Melissa is humiliated, but Stu is free.

I bring this up as an example of taking a character to the next level. In Stu's case, what's worse than a domineering, pain in the ass girlfriend? A domineering, pain in the ass girlfriend who actually lacks the genuine moral superiority to mistreat Stu. Knowing that she had sex with the bartender on a cruise ship makes her an even more unlikable character, and we experience a certain gratification when we see Stu dump Melissa. Without adding that step and informing the audience about Melissa's infidelity, she would have only been an annoying girlfriend. That one piece of additional information makes Stu's story a more satisfying one.

NOTE: At this point, I received another question from a different writer who said she would soon be writing a screenplay, and wanted me to guide her through the process of diving deeper into a main character. I really didn't want to go there because this kind of work takes time, more time than I wanted to devote to it in a class setting. Without an appropriate amount of time allotted to the exercise, the last thing I would want is for people in attendance to be underwhelmed with the results, because I truly believe in the character-layering procedure.

Before answering, I asked the writer to tell me what her main character's occupation is so that I could weigh my options. She said he's a cop, specifically a Detective assigned to Narcotics. I thought, what the hell? Let's do this!

Okay, here goes. Cops are one of the characters we see most in movies, and I suspect it's because cops are people we see all the time in our real lives. You see them on the road patrolling the streets, on the news, everywhere. It doesn't matter where you live, you've got cops nearby. We can relate to them, and they aren't strangers in our communities. They are civil servants, and our taxes pay their salaries. Some people trust them and call them when they're in trouble, while others distrust them and consider cops to be the source of conflict. Cops carry badges and guns, and that gives them a kind of power and authority that the rest of us don't have and can't wield.

We've all seen countless cop movies, and it's hard to imagine how yet another film about a cop wouldn't be some type of rehash of a cop character we've already seen. Think about all the things cops, regardless of where they're from, have in common. The uniforms and firearms, the training, the long hours and tough schedules they work, the creeps they encounter on the job, the chases, the gun battles, the fist fights, difficult relationships with loved ones, the constant risks and danger, the psychological stress, etc. The cops in most cities, and even small towns face many of the same issues. So, to make your cop interesting and new, you'll need to look beyond the typical characteristics they already share and seek unique qualities elsewhere. Consider factors that might not have initially been included in the plans for your particular character. What I recommend is taking the character to a new place in your head and continually interrogating them about their actions and emotions.

Based on what this student said in class, we know her main character is a Detective, but she went on to say that he's a veteran undercover cop assigned to a narcotics detail. He was well respected in the department up until recently, when he was accused by the major drug dealer he busted of stealing money and illegal drugs during the raid. The cop's career might be over, and worse, he could be on his way to prison. The writer then went on to tell me that her main character, the cop, really did steal the money and cash from the drug dealer. The cop broke the law. He is guilty. When I asked the writer why the cop did it, considering he was a hero in the department, she told me he needed the money and had no other way to get it. But that's all she knew for sure! He did it, because he had to. I can see where a lot of new writers would think that was enough to know in order to start in on a script about this character, but I couldn't disagree more.

For the purpose of this explanation, it doesn't really matter how the writer's story turned out. What is important is that I forced her to ask questions that she didn't know the answers to. She soon figured out why the cop stole the money and drugs, but we also ran through so many other possibilities that it gave her even more story information she could use in her script. The cop was going to be investigated, and it would help to know what all the theories might be as to why he committed the crime.

This is the simple drill that gave the writer more clarity. I asked the questions, she answered. Here's how it went:

Why would a cop who was considered trustworthy and a hero to his fellow officers and community ever give in to temptation and take cash and illegal drugs from a crime scene? Did he get fed up and resent the system? No.

Did he catch other cops stealing and feel that if he didn't take part in it, they would forever fear that he would turn them in? No.

Was he broke or just more broke than other cops? No. Sure, money was tight, but he wasn't broke.

Why was money tight? Did he have a big family? No. Just one kid. Was his wife spending more than he could afford, but he couldn't get her to stop? No.

All right, so he apparently needed more money than he was earning. What did he need extra money for? It must've been very important, if he was willing to be kicked off the force and go to jail for it. Was he a gambler? No. Was he a drug addict? No. Did he owe money to a loan shark? No.

Was he going to be retiring soon? No. You know, there are some cops who give the best years of their lives to their job, putting their lives on the line and taking shit from criminals every day and then, when it's time to get their pension, they feel like they've been short-changed. Is it possible that this hero cop wanted a little something extra to see him through his golden years? No.

Did he promise his wife that he'd take her on a second honeymoon? No. Did he want to run away? Disappear and start his life over again someplace else? No. Was he leading some kind of secret life, maybe with a child and another woman? No. Was he having an affair and he needed cash to keep it going? No. Was he being blackmailed? No.

Okay, this is crazy, but did he do it just for the thrill of it? No. It doesn't sound like the money was for him, which means it was for someone else and a hero cop like this guy wouldn't be willing to throw his life away unless it was for someone very important to him.

There are all kinds of possibilities here. Does he have a kid in college and if the cop doesn't get his hands on some quick cash, the kid won't be able to finish their education? No.

The rest of the stuff I'm thinking about is too frivolous, like promising to buy his son or daughter a car. No, it can't be anything like that. An expense like that isn't something you go to prison for, unless you're beyond desperate, so forget that.

Does he have a family member who is in trouble? Let's take this path. Yes. His son. He's 24 years old. Is he in some kind of legal trouble? Does he need to pay for his son's lawyer to keep him out of prison? No. Does he need to bribe someone, like a Judge? No. Did his son borrow money from a gangster who will kill him if he doesn't pay it back? No. Is his son having some type of health issue? Yes. He needs to go to rehab for drug addiction. Okay, but the cop is a long-time city employee, which means he has to be provided with health insurance and the kid is under 26, which means he can still be on his father's policy. Yes, that's true. Thank you, Obamacare! So, if his son needs rehab and he has insurance, then there must be another reason the cop needs a lot of cash to pay for it. I think I got it. Is it important that nobody knows the cop's son is in rehab? Yes. Bingo!

But I'm not finished. Why is it a secret that the cop's son is in rehab? A lot of people go to rehab for all kinds of things, so why is this a problem? I think we would all agree that, when someone has a problem with any type of addiction, going to rehab is a good thing. Is it because the cop doesn't want to have to explain to anyone how a big narcotics cop's son ends up a drug addict, which kind of suggests that the cop is a bad father? No. So, it's not an ego thing. No, not like that. The only other reason I can think of for not wanting to let the rehab be billed by insurance, which means people will find out about it, is because someone will be very embarrassed by this news getting out. Yes. Friends wouldn't care, a sibling who loves his or her brother might care. But I'm guessing it's his Mom who doesn't want anyone to know. Yes. It makes sense. She will be perceived as a bad mother, and her son will be smeared in the eyes of the public. It's best that no one know.

I can only imagine the kind of pressure that was dropped on this cop's shoulders by his wife, to make him cross the line and become a criminal. Everything he worked for, and everything he is, could be lost in a moment of justifiable weakness. I can understand that he loves his son and wants what's best for him. I can understand that he loves his wife too. But this is extreme. There must be a very bizarre dynamic in the relationship between the cop and his wife, because my wife would never expect me to do something like this to avoid embarrassment.

Consider what they will have to go through now as a family, because the cop's wife thinks it was more important to keep up appearances in the neighborhood than remain a law abiding, righteous, veteran cop. But we're still not finished.

What is the aftermath within the family now that the cop has been arrested? Some thought should be given to these concerns. In addition, why did the cop steal the drugs? Remember the facts. Our veteran narcotics cop stole the cash and the drugs. The money aspect has been treated to a fair amount of theorizing, but what would the cop want with the illegal drugs? Is the cop going to sell the drugs for additional cash? Unlikely. Will he sock the drugs away as an emergency source of funds? Risky and dumb. Is the cop going to destroy the drugs to keep them off the streets? An idealist would do that. All of these choices are legitimate. The only thing I would say you can count on as being impossible is that the cop would ever give the drugs to his son, the addict.

As you can imagine, our discussion of this main character went on for some time, and numerous possibilities were explored. An incredible amount of useful information was mined from students in the class in a matter of minutes. But at some point, the writing of your screenplay must begin. Until that time comes, jump into this process and get to know your characters better than you know most people in your daily life.

QUESTION SIX

LEARNING TO LOVE THE ROPE

How much rewriting should we really expect to do? I like my screenplay the way it is, I worked really hard on it, and I want to see how people react to it before I make any changes.

I happen to be one of those people who likes to rewrite a script more than I like writing the original draft. I always find something I want to change, maybe I've stumbled onto a better idea or two, or I've decided that something needs to come out because it doesn't work as well as I had hoped or intended. Perhaps someone I trust has given me food for thought, and I'm willing to give my new perspective a shot. It can be a minor reworking or a full-blown rewrite from Page 1, but whatever it is, I can honestly say I always look forward to making improvements to my scripts, especially after I've made such a big investment of time and trouble in it up to this point. Regardless of the motivation, rewriting is a mandatory process that aspiring professional writers should embrace.

Unfortunately, I find that a surprisingly large percentage of writers I meet hate the idea and process of rewriting. They consider it a torturous procedure, not a golden opportunity to turn a good script into a great one. Honestly, I don't get it. How can someone claim that they want to be a writer if they don't see a rewrite as a natural and necessary extension of their initial efforts on a screenplay?

Here's some truth, folks. Rewriting is not a luxury, it's a non-negotiable component of writing, and the more you do it, the more skillful you will become. I hate to admit this, but when I was first starting out, I didn't think I needed to rewrite my scripts. They were great the way they were, and who would know that better than the writer? Part of it was pure stubbornness, part of it was over-anxiousness, part of it was the silliness or stupidity that comes with being a rank amateur and part of it was unadulterated ego. I didn't want to hear, from anyone, that my script needed some work. What I wasn't considering back then is how foolish it is to devote many months to writing a script, while being unwilling to spend a few weeks on making it better. I'm grateful that I understand that now and that I've outgrown such a ridiculous stance, and I urge other writers to expand their horizons and make that same move. A writer who refuses to rewrite is his or her own worst enemy.

First drafts are invariably full of errors. You're in "create mode" and you might not be able to spot the typos or formatting mistakes simply because you've looked at the same pages dozens of times, but they're there, and I'll bet you anything a reader will zero in on them. Your story could be near perfect, if there is such a thing, but the minor clerical blunders will add up and identify you as an amateur. A reader might reach the conclusion that a writer who can't spell, especially when software will correct most typos, can't possible know how to properly structure a story. Don't give a reader the ammunition with which to shoot down your script.

When I talk about rewriting, I'm not only referring to fixing the kinds of mistakes I just mentioned. You've quite possibly got bigger fish to fry, but the good news is that you've already done the hardest part of the work. You came up with a story and you pounded out the first draft of a screenplay. That's a significant accomplishment to be proud of, and now's the time to take it to the next level.

Keep in mind, as a disembodied, recurring pep talk, that even Oscar-winning screenwriters rewrite their scripts, over and over again. Even an A-list writer's first draft is never a shooting script. It's a fact of life. If you are fortunate enough to sell a screenplay, you will very quickly discover that the number of rewrites is only limited by time. A studio or producer will insist on a given number of rewrites and polishes, some of which you might be asked to do yourself, based on the terms set out in your contract. But whatever the scenario, get the faulty idea out of your mind that screams your script is good just the way it is and doesn't need more work. Once you get accustomed to the rewriting process, and you do it religiously, you will eventually begin to sense when you've done your last pass. In the meantime, keep chasing the illusion of the perfect script.

A word of wisdom: Wait until you've completed your first draft before you begin to rewrite. A common trap that new writers fall into is going back over Act One, rewriting it time and again. If you insist on doing this, you will never get to the end of your screenplay. This is a form of avoidance. Keep the forward momentum going, and wait until after you've written "The End" before you start on the rewrite.

A second word of wisdom: When you set out to rewrite, don't race for the finish line. A rush job will bring little, if any additional value to your script. I remember writing an episode of "Tales from the Crypt" for my agent to use as a sample. I came up with a good story, banged out the pages, then dropped it off at his office. It was very early in my career, and I honestly, and foolishly, expected my agent to call me and tell me that it was perfect as is, and that he already submitted it to several producers of several shows, and that I could expect to have multiple job offers within a matter of a day or two. Instead, he called to tell me that it needed a little work. I was deflated, but defiant. We discussed it, and I recall disagreeing with him on most of his notes. He just didn't get it. I agreed to do the rewrite, begrudgingly. I launched into it right away, and delivered the rewritten script to my agent the following day. He was stunned, but not in a good way. While I thought he would be impressed at how quickly I performed the rewrite, the opposite was true. He refused to believe that I took his suggestions seriously, and he was right. It took me a few more years to realize that speed isn't what's important when doing a rewrite. The process should be undertaken with the intent to make positive changes to your work, and any approach that isn't likely to address all of the problem areas can't achieve your goal.

Rewriting is not torture, or at least it doesn't have to be. I like to say that writers who resist it need to learn to love the rope. That expression comes from a low budget movie from 1977 called "Rolling Thunder," written by Paul Schrader and starring William Devane. In that film, a Vietnam War P.O.W. finally comes home after spending years in a North Vietnamese prison camp where he was brutally tortured in a variety of gruesome ways. Once home, he demonstrates one of the methods frequently used on him, and it consists of having his arms tied tightly behind his back, at which point his tormentors would use the rope to hoist his arms up in the air behind his back while they beat him. When asked how he could possibly endure such horrible abuse and suffering day after day, he replied, "You learn to love the rope." In other words, once you no longer perceive the torture as being unpleasant, the enemy can no longer hurt you with it. You've beaten them at their own game.

For those who don't believe in the immense benefits of rewriting, I would urge you to learn to love the rope. It isn't painful unless you allow it to be. Maybe one day, it will become something you look forward to doing.

QUESTION SEVEN

SCRIPT TITLE

I don't exactly have writer's block, but I do find myself getting bogged down with details that keep me from moving forward in my script. For example, the title. How important is it for me to have a title for my movie, and won't the buyer eventually change it anyway?

Please allow me to remove some of the unnecessary stress that seems to be plaguing you. You definitely don't need a permanent title for your screenplay while you're in the writing process. First of all, who will see it at that stage, aside from you? When you come up with a title you really like, go ahead and plug it in. Then again, if it fails to pop into your head along the way, don't panic. You can always refer to your Buddy Cop Comedy script as "Untitled Buddy Cop Comedy." I feel comfortable in saying that you can even use a temporary, working title when giving the screenplay to your agent or industry reader.

Of course, if you can devise a title that adds a measure of excitement and cleverness to the script, that's a plus. Anything you can do to give your project more shine is a smart move. But if you can only manage a so-so working title, use it. If the script is praiseworthy, no one is going to temper their interest just because they aren't in love with the title. And yes, a buyer may very well change the title, as is their right. But that would mean there's a buyer, and you should be thrilled with the sale of your script, new title or not. In that case, all of your agonizing was for nothing. Let's not forget that the original title of "Pretty Woman" was "3000" and Woody Allen's "Annie Hall" was "Anhedonia." Go ahead, exhale and get back to work.

QUESTION EIGHT

MAIN CHARACTERS

Can you give me a basic rundown of the different kinds of main characters that need to be included in my script? Hero/protagonist, villain/antagonist, mentor, friend/ally, etc.?

Of course, I can. But I won't, for good reasons. A very clear, concise and complete version of what you're requesting already exists. I urge every writer I meet, whether they ask or not, to log onto Amazon or go to the local bookstore ASAP to get a copy of a guide that I truly believe does the best job I've ever seen of explaining various character archetypes. It's called "The Writer's Journey" by Christopher Vogler.

I vividly recall the first time I read it in one very pleasurable and enlightening sitting, many years ago, and feeling like I finally understood concepts that had eluded me. Sometimes, it's difficult to fully grasp the significance of a specific character type, especially in the abstract. When Mr. Vogler uses examples from well-known films, the light in a writer's head tends to go on and stay on.

I'm sure some smart-alecks will think I'm copping out and that I just don't want to go to all the trouble of explaining the major and minor character types that inhabit every good story ever told. That's baloney, and to be respectful of Italian screenwriters, bologna. I teach my seminars to provide writers with the best and most comprehensive education I can provide over a very intense and condensed period of time, and I'm more than capable of breaking down characters, but I'm also not delusional. The truth is, I cannot improve on what Mr. Vogler has already made available to you. "The Writer's Journey" is easily digestible and his elucidations are still amazingly fresh in my mind. Read his book, and all your questions will likely be answered.

By the way, as long as I'm recommending screenwriting books and you're going online or to the bookstore, grab William Goldman's classic "Adventures in the Screen Trade." While you may not immediately recognize his name, you will definitely know his work. Mr. Goldman wrote some of my all-time favorite movies like "The Princess Bride," "Misery," "All the President's Men," "Butch Cassidy and the Sundance Kid," "Papillon," "Marathon Man," and many more. He's one of my industry heroes and you can learn an awful lot about writing and the industry simply by reading his story about the first time a studio executive asked Mr. Goldman to write a dialogue-free opening credit sequence for "Harper." The movie is from the 1960s; it's great fun and I still think of it every time I make coffee.

QUESTION NINE

SILLY THINGS WRITERS SAY

I've noticed that guidelines and formats for scripts can vary depending on who you ask and which book you read, and it's confusing. Newer books on screenwriting have very different rules than the older books that have been around forever, yet instructors or speakers refer to all of them. In my case, I have a retired writer telling me that my script can't exceed 120 pages, but a magazine article I read said 110 pages is the maximum. Are either of those numbers accurate? The script I'm almost done with is already 131 pages, with probably another 15 to go, but it can't be cut down without losing important story points.

This is one of my all-time favorite questions, but not because it's about page counts today versus page counts of yesteryear. As a matter of fact, I have a separate chapter that specifically addresses the length of feature scripts. No, I absolutely love this question because the writer boldly announces that his script, which exceeds all of the industry standards he mentioned, cannot be trimmed down without severely hurting the story. Wow. Your story is so damn remarkable and so fabulous, not to mention well-written, that you can't afford to lose a word here and there without doing irreparable harm? Bullshit. Not uncommon, but still bullshit.

Are you telling me that if an executive from Warner Brothers flipped head over heels for your script and wanted to buy it today, but only if it came in at 117 1/2 pages on the dot, you still wouldn't be able to make any cuts? If so, I want to wish you a lot of luck in Hollywood. Scripts are written, and then rewritten, ad nauseam. What makes you so special that your pages are untouchable? If you can't bear to do revisions or make cuts that entail shortening or editing out scenes or dialogue, you're going to have a hard time working as a writer. When I was just starting out, I heard one experienced writer after another say, in one way or another, that they don't get married to their material, but only to their spouse. I learned how important it is to abide by that philosophy and limit the amount of unnecessary stress I would otherwise create for myself.

It's crazy, but I get very excited whenever I hear this type of question because it's the perfect introduction to my list of silly things that writers should never say out loud, especially if they're within earshot of producers, studio and network executives, or agents.

SILLY THINGS WRITERS SAY... TO PROVE THEY ARE AMATEURS:

1. My script is so awesome, it can't be limited to 120 pages.
2. The well-established rules of screenwriting don't apply to me.
3. My story is so complicated, in a good way, that a logline simply can't describe it.
4. I don't like the way 12-point Courier font looks on the page, so I use Century Gothic. It's cool!
5. I mailed a copy of my script to myself, which means it's protected by Copyright law.
6. A producer says he loves my script but he wants me to do some rewrites on it for free before he decides if he wants to buy it. Oh, yeah. And we don't have any kind of agreement yet, but he wants me to get started on it right away and said he would give me a contract later, if it sells.

7. I know a retired personal injury attorney in Cottonwood Falls who says he can get my screenplay to all the big studios.
8. I mailed my script to a bunch of producers in L.A., without them asking, and I still haven't heard back from any of them. It's been about three months, so should I call them?
9. I met Kareem Abdul Jabbar's publicist at a car wash and gave him a copy of a script that I had in the trunk. He said Kareem doesn't really want to do movies, but if I can get my script set up at a major studio, he'd talk to Erik Estrada about starring in it.
10. I went to a big pitch festival last summer and eight different producers said they really loved my ideas and screenplays. It's been eleven months and nothing has happened yet, but they probably got busy. I hope to see them at the next pitch festival I registered for.
11. I paid three different companies to read my script and give me coverage, and all of them said it was either fair or good. One of them even checked the box that said "Recommend!"
12. You don't understand. I can't change my story because those things really happened to me!

I know that this list is a little bit humbling and maybe a tad embarrassing, because all of you have uttered at least one or two of these cringe-worthy statements. I know I did when I was just starting out and thought I knew what the hell I was talking about. The good news is that all is not permanently lost. Learn from your mistakes, mature as a writer, commit to doing your best work, and once you can sound and behave like a professional, stake your claim as a member of the entertainment industry community.

QUESTION TEN

IMDB

If a producer or a production entity likes my screenplay, but they see that I don't have any credits on IMDB, will that hurt my chances of getting them to take me seriously and buy my script?

I don't usually answer a question with a question, but this is one of those situations where I think it will help me to make a point you will hopefully remember.

Let's pretend you're a biomechanical engineer and you just invented a brand spanking new artificial heart valve that will revolutionize the field of medicine and save countless lives around the world. When researchers and manufacturers test it and it checks out as the best-ever product of its kind, do you think the mega-businessmen who are going to sell your device for billions of dollars will ask to see your college grades? Will the acceptance of your game-changing invention by the medical technology industry depend on what kind of successful or failed projects you worked on five years ago? If your new partners will corner the market and change the field of cardiology forever, are they going to want to know who your girlfriend was at Stanford, whether you worked at Burger King during high school, or if you have ever sold any homemade gadgets before?

I think you know what I'm getting at. If the executives at a movie studio can make hundreds of millions of dollars with your screenplay, they won't care about what you wrote ten years ago—or if you've ever written anything before. You could have written the script for the "Worst Movie of the Year" award at the Razzies, and all will be forgiven if your new script is awesome, marketable and above all, profitable. I sometimes feel like you could be functionally illiterate and resort to dictating your script to an assistant, and still sell your screenplay if a fantastic, funny filmmaker like Judd Apatow reads it and wants it to be his next hit.

If you don't currently have any credits on IMDB, but your script kicks the proverbial ass, then your absence from the website won't hurt your cause. By the same token, if you have 25 good credits on IMDB, but you've written an atrocious script this time around, you'll find out very quickly just how much those past credits are worth when you're trying to sell a piece of garbage today. Not a heck of a lot.

I don't know when IMDB came into existence but I do know that I started earning a living as a screenwriter in the late 1980's before the internet was available to civilians and before you could size me up on IMDB. In 30 years, not a single agent or executive has ever asked me a single question about what they've seen on my IMDB profile. In fact, I've never heard a writer say IMDB has had a positive or negative effect on their career.

In my opinion, writers, especially those outside L.A., are far too fascinated with IMDB. The only time I even look at IMDB is when I can't remember the name of a character actor I liked in a movie or TV series from a few decades ago. It's the perfect tool when it comes to digging up miscellaneous factoids or interesting stories, but as for whether it can prevent you from having a career as a writer, I think you should rest at ease and rely on my assessment that it is totally inconsequential. If you're inspired to read the gospel, pick up a Bible and save IMDB for when you're competing in a trivia contest and you can't remember who played Peggy on "Mannix." It's Gail Fisher.

One final thought about IMDB. While it's a great resource for some people in the industry, it's extremely difficult to get the website to add, delete, and change information on your profile. This is based on my own frustrating experience over many years. Not only is there erroneous information in my bio, but over the course of three decades as a professional writer, I've amassed three pages of credits for TV and film projects I've Written and/or Produced, and only a handful of them appear on my official IMDB filmography. I've tried, oh how I've tried, repeatedly, to have IMDB remove the silliness from my bio, and have made every effort to convince them to add the vast majority of my produced credits to my profile, but to no avail. Don't get me wrong. I am not suggesting that IMDB is an evil empire. Not at all. There's no conspiracy operating there. It does fulfill a certain purpose. However, it's important to remember that no one website on the internet is unerringly thorough or complete.

My advice is: stop worrying about IMDB and write a great script.

QUESTION ELEVEN

PARTNERS

I've been writing some TV scripts with a friend of mine, and we'd like to submit them as samples. Is it easier to get a job as a team or as individuals with separate samples?

It's never easy to get a writing job, period. God only knows how many extremely talented people have tried everything under the sun, but never succeeded at getting hired. You may never know why it happens or doesn't happen, but it should be obvious that the writers who keep writing through the rejection and refuse to give up have a better shot at getting their turn.

When it comes to landing a TV writing gig, I would also never say it's easier to get a job doing things one way versus another. Count on this: your writing sample will do most of the talking for you. Like I always say, it's impossible to know why someone makes the cut and someone else doesn't. There are so many variables to consider. How many available writing positions are there on a given show? Are they looking for someone with a lot of experience or are they willing to take a chance on a new writer? Are they under unspoken pressure from the office down the hall to fill a vacancy with a male writer, a female writer, a writer from a specific racial group, or a writer with a specific sexual orientation or gender identity? Have the powers that be promised the next available writing job to an assistant who, up until now, has been primarily responsible for making coffee, picking up the Executive Producer's dry cleaning and driving the star's car to the airport, leaving it with a valet, and taking the bus back to the office? Or, my personal favorite. Does the creator of the series have a nephew or cousin or in-law that has always wanted to be a TV writer? If so, it may not matter how fantastic your sample script is. You see, your only chance at getting that writing position vanished into thin air when your sister refused a marriage proposal from the showrunner's brother. If you're laughing at the ridiculousness of that scenario or shaking your head in disbelief, then you haven't spent enough time in Los Angeles. I have personally witnessed all of those hiring variations take place.

Before I continue to answer this question, let me take a brief detour that will illustrate a different, but related, point. Getting a TV writing job isn't a cake walk under the best of circumstances. There are a veritable army of new writers who manage to land their first gig through hard work, persistence and luck, but who never get the second opportunity. Despite their best efforts, the well dries up as quickly as they struck oil the first time around. I have a friend who came to L.A. from Alabama for a shot at a writing career. He got his foot in the door without much difficulty, however, he was never able to duplicate that first break. After years of pounding away on his computer keyboard and the doors of countless producers, to no avail, he finally quit the business and moved back to Dixieland. My point is that getting a writing position on a TV show isn't the end of the struggle, it's the beginning.

When it comes to writing for a living, and as is the case in any business, a superior product speaks for itself. If you have a strong sample of your work to use as a calling card, the odds are much better that you will get the attention of those in charge. But if your material is questionable, the chances of having a positive outcome are slim. While you may be very entertaining and charming in meetings, you won't likely have an opportunity to speak with the boss unless your sample stands out from the rest.

From your question, I assume that you and your friend are hoping to work together as a writing team on a TV show. There are many such teams and it isn't unusual for a show to want to hire a team when they can. After all, the network might be able to get two good writers for the price of one. The deal of course, would be negotiated by your representative, so the financial aspect of that kind of arrangement shouldn't concern you too much. But what a lot of writers don't know is that, under the WGA rules, a writing team cannot be created or dissolved by any external entity. Only the writers themselves can initiate or terminate a partnership. Therefore, producers cannot force two individual writers to become a team, nor can they break up a team that is already in existence, electing to keep one writer while dismissing the other. In a nutshell, if you are hired together, you are fired together, if that day should ever come.

Believe it or not, I witnessed that very thing happen to two good friends of mine who were brought onto the staff of a sitcom as a writing team. One of them was brash, the other soft-spoken, but both were funny and talented writers. One day, after a particularly brutal session in the writers' room, my friends were summoned to the Executive Producer's office. He told the two writers that during the session, he noticed that the brash writer rolled his eyes at a joke the Executive Producer pitched. His ego bruised, the EP wanted to fire the writer who failed to acknowledge the hilarity of the alleged joke. While he really liked the more mild-mannered writer, his hands were tied by the WGA. My buddies were hired as a team and he was prohibited from getting rid of one and keeping the other. As a result, both were unceremoniously canned right then and there. There are two lessons to be learned from this true story: 1) Only partner up with someone whose behavior is in line with your own, and 2) Learn to laugh at everything the EP says, no matter how lame his or her jokes are.

When I was offered my first TV writing job, I was told that the head honcho couldn't decide between hiring me or another fledgling writer. He liked us both, wanted us both on staff, but even though the show was a big hit and was generating millions of dollars in revenue, he insisted that he didn't have the budget necessary to hire us both. The only way I could be guaranteed the position was to agree to team up with the other writer, who was a guy I had never even met before. I didn't want to do it, but my agent insisted that I not miss out on the chance of a lifetime. I took the job and met my writing partner at a hastily arranged dinner that night. The credits for the series could have referred to us as the writing team of Oil & Water, because that's about how well we mixed. At the end of my 13-week contract, I was let go and my partner was renewed. If you've been paying attention, you'll recognize that the EP didn't just violate the union rules by making us work as a team, but he did it again when he didn't pick up my contract, but still kept my partner on staff. I probably would've complained to the WGA if it hadn't been for the fact that I was hired onto another show about two weeks later. I found the silver lining to that cloud, but many others never do. By the way, I found out several years later that my agent at the time had lied, and that I didn't have to agree to the writing team arrangement to get the job. He simply wanted to get work for two clients instead of one. Hooray for Hollywood!

There's absolutely nothing wrong with teaming up. I would recommend however, that you know the rules, follow the rules, and only partner with someone you actually know in your civilian life and want to work with.

QUESTION TWELVE

SHOULD I HAVE A PARTNER?

In general, are you for or against having a writing partner?

If you're asking this question, I would guess that you're concerned about writing with a partner for one of these reasons. You've been planning to work with someone, but are feeling apprehensive that having a partner manufactures more trouble than it's worth. Perhaps you've already started a project together and you're worried about where it's heading or what kinds of problems are hiding in the bad idea dumpster right around the corner. Or you're hoping I will advise you to work with a partner because someone else will be responsible for carrying at least half of the workload, while also providing other benefits you will enjoy from having a second set of brain cells at your disposal. I will do my best to answer this from the perspective of someone who has worked with a partner on a few occasions, but who spent most of his career writing on his own.

I think most of it comes down to who your partner is and what they believe a partnership should be. Are they someone who likes to freely collaborate? Are you? Is there something about their writing ability that might be missing from your own bag of tricks? Are you looking for someone stronger and more disciplined than you are, who will do their share of writing while also keeping your butt in the chair? Are they a creative powerhouse, and might they overpower you and routinely dismiss your contributions? Is this someone you can spend a lot of time with, day in and day out, under intense pressure? And how well do they function in that same pressure cooker? Are they good with deadlines? Do they have annoying habits that might drive you nuts? If they're a smoker, will they want to take a cigarette or vaping break every fifteen minutes? If they're a drinker, will they cease to be of value after a few beers – and they always seem to have a few beers while they are working with you? Do they have a thin skin or quick temper? Are they of the opposite sex, and will that cause a problem with temptation, not to mention a big area of concern for your spouse or significant other? Is your potential partner willing to work on the script on a predetermined, regular schedule as you are, or can they only devote a few hours to it every now and then when they have spare time?

Before having a serious discussion with your prospective partner, I would suggest that you pose these kinds of questions to yourself, and then pay close attention to your own responses. If your gut tells you that you're asking for a disastrous outcome or that your script writing process will be hampered by having a partner, maybe you should skip it. If you are still wanting to proceed with a partner, I wouldn't be shy about asking some or most of those same questions to your prime candidates. After all, they may have the same kind of uncertainty about you and your strengths and weaknesses.

Talk about these questions together, openly and honestly, pro and con, and see where it leads. If you are afraid to broach the subject for fear that your potential partner will be offended, that speaks volumes. Imagine what it will be like when you encounter an actual obstacle while working together, instead of just asking a possibly uncomfortable question.

I would recommend that you consider these types of factors at the earliest phase of your exploration into working with a partner, before you jump headlong into a situation or relationship where ideas are being pitched easily among you and your prospective writing partner, or other writers in general. Not to be an alarmist, but based on my personal experience, I can tell you that even the most innocent set of circumstances can provide fertile ground in which disputes will grow and eventually blossom into ugliness.

For example, pretend you're having a friendly dinner with another writer. What if a good idea is the unintended product of a discussion over dessert? Who does that idea belong to? What if you want to write it but you want to do so on your own? What if the other writer is possessive when it comes to every word that comes out of his mouth, valuable or not? What if the other party insists on writing it with you but they have no experience, no knowledge of screenwriting techniques, no talent, and no discipline? Is that someone you would like to be handcuffed to while writing the script? If possible, avoid situations that will compromise your work as a writer.

Believe it or not, it can get even worse. What if you are sitting with another writer and you feel comfortable pitching them your favorite idea, and they are so incredibly inspired by your original story that before you can stop them, they begin to blurt out their own unsolicited ideas for scenes, locations or characters that they think would help your script? If you're very lucky, they really only intended to openly share their thoughts with you, one writer to another, and that's fine. But what if they believe you have invited them to write with you simply because you remained silent as they pitched their ideas, and they now expect to write the script with you just because they contributed unwanted, unsolicited ideas? Yes, there are people like that and when you remind them that you didn't ask them for their comments, they will go so far as to threaten to sue you if you dare to use any of their fantastic ideas. What if you already had similar ideas before the discussion? Will they believe that or, in the alternative, accuse you of wanting to steal their brilliant musings? Honestly, who needs that kind of headache?

If you are going to write with a partner, my advice is that you immediately compose and sign an agreement that spells out the terms of your writing partnership, and be paranoid, please. Don't leave anything out. Do it before you have your first serious chat about the project, and definitely prior to writing anything, including FADE IN. The more you can agree to in advance, in writing, the less likelihood that there will be disagreements and misunderstandings later.

It doesn't have to be a formal contract written in legalese. You don't need to pay a lawyer to draft it. If you aren't confident about what you're composing, do a Google search for "collaboration agreement" and get some actual samples, then customize your agreement to suit the needs of you and your partner. It would only take me a few seconds to find several collaboration agreement templates online, and list the links here, but I'm not the one looking to partner up. You are. Take my advice, do a minute of research and protect yourself.

When you know what you want to draft, put together a memo that describes what you will be working on with your partner and what will happen if things go south at some point in the future. For example, what happens if you are in the middle of writing Act Two of your screenplay, and your partner no longer agrees on the direction the story should take from that point forward? If you don't include a provision in your agreement that spells out how those disagreements will be resolved, you may very well end up with a half-written script that no one owns, and that will never be completed. You should also be sure to include the steps that you will take once the script is finished. What is the game plan you both agree to abide by? The last thing you need, after working so hard on a screenplay, is to argue about how to best approach the task of getting it into the right hands.

The truth is, answering this question about partnerships is giving me a stomachache, and that should tell you something. Speaking only for myself, my writing partnership experiences weren't all nightmares, but they weren't exactly rainbows and lollipops either. I once had an otherwise productive and friendly partnership fall apart simply because we couldn't agree on when to work. I also had a TV deal disintegrate because my partner spoke so rudely to the Executive Producers, they never wanted to talk to us about the project again. I quickly apologized for his conduct, and my personal and work relationship with those Execs has remained intact to this day, but that's how little it takes to sink a show that you worked very hard to set up.

For me, writing with a partner, more often than not, turned out to be a negative transaction, and trying it again isn't something near the top of my bucket list. Don't get me wrong. Many writing partnerships are wildly successful. Some of the best movies and TV shows ever made were written by teams. I just know that it isn't for me, and I would caution anyone with even the slightest misgivings about it to listen to their heart and dodge the bullet. If you should decide that a writing partnership is for you, so be it. Get going on that script, but remember to get that agreement signed first!

QUESTION THIRTEEN

CAN I SELL A SCRIPT

I live about 600 miles away from Los Angeles and I've only been writing for about a year and a half. Is it realistic to think that someone like me can sell a screenplay to a movie studio or production company, or am I just kidding myself and wasting my time?

The best way for me to answer your question is to ask you a question of my own. Do you think all the good ideas for movies coincidentally come from people who already live in the Hollywood area? Of course not. Yes, L.A. is filled to the rafters with writers. But so is the rest of the world. The point is, anyone is capable of coming up with a great idea, and I truly believe anyone can sell a script. It just needs to be fantastic in just about every way and it must be professionally written. So, what are you going to do about it?

I would say the main difference between the writers in Los Angeles, especially those who have moved here to pursue a career in the industry, and the writers I meet around the country, is that the writers in L.A. seem to be more committed to writing their script and finding a way, when they're done, to get it into the right hands and noticed by those who ultimately make the important decisions that directly impact a writer's existence. Many of the L.A. writers feel that they have no choice but to give it their best shot. They don't have a Plan B, and that takes a lot of guts. Writers outside of L.A. are usually writing in their spare time or as a hobby. Many of them have the luxury of not needing to make a dime from writing because they have a job, a place to live, food on the table, etc. If they never write anything worth a damn, their life won't feel like a disaster. They took a shot, it didn't work out, and they're fine. But when you relocate to L.A. to make it big, and you tell everyone you meet that you're a writer, it's exponentially more devastating when you can't get any traction on any of your projects. It's romantic to be a starving artist, but when you're eating Top Ramen every night for dinner and can't pay your bills, being a struggling screenwriter doesn't stay sexy for long.

If you have a marketable idea, along with some talent and self-discipline, it doesn't matter where you live. When I teach my seminars in various cities around the country, I meet would-be writers who come out of the theater, just like professional writers in L.A., and say, "Damn it, that movie sucked. How do I get those two hours of my life back? My ideas are so much better than that!" If that sounds like you, don't be embarrassed. Every writer I know says the same thing, including me. The only difference is that some writers use that frustration as motivation to get to work and keep their nose to the grindstone until their script is done. Other writers have been working on the same Act One since Bush was President. Bush 41, not 43. So, again, what are you going to do about it?

The first logical step is to make a major decision. Will you consistently devote as much time as you can to outlining, writing and rewriting your script? If the answer is yes, then step two is easy. Do it! I can guarantee you that, if you don't do the work, nothing good will happen. If you are willing to do what it takes to write a screenplay, and execute it properly, then yes, you can manufacture an opportunity to have it read by the people who count. Start right now, if you haven't already. Read as many relevant scripts as you can, plan out every aspect of your story, chain yourself to your desk, if necessary, and get it done. Never forget that show business is just that. It's a business, and as my father used to say, nobody is in business with the goal of going out of business. First and foremost, the people who make movies also want to make money. If you write an awesome screenplay and they feel that they can cash in on it, they'll buy it, and trust me, they won't give a hoot in hell where you're from.

QUESTION FOURTEEN

THE USE OF PROFANITY

What are the rules when it comes to using profanity in a screenplay—and will it hurt my chances at impressing a studio executive because I used foul language?

I consider this to be a particularly good question because it gives me an opportunity to address the issue of language and profanity, but not just in the way you raised it.

When it comes to the use of profanity in a script, I've always used whatever language I felt was necessary to communicate the way my character would actually speak in any given situation. Doesn't that make sense as the only way to write dialogue? I've never censored a character when to do so would take away the words he or she would employ to communicate authentically. When writing a character's dialogue, you should keep in mind who they are, what they're like, where they are, what they're doing, and what the context is. Whatever comes out of a character's mouth shouldn't sound like anyone else, but only because it sounds exactly like them, the person you've created! If it isn't genuine, delete it.

We live in the real world, full of real people who speak in ways that might make us uncomfortable at times. If you're easily offended by "dirty words" in your daily life, you may have a tough time using them in your scripts. But if you pay close attention to the way the average person speaks, man or woman, rich or poor, black or white, young or old, etc., you're bound to notice, very quickly, that profanity is everywhere. I've never had a problem with it and I doubt that any studio executive will either, unless you've gone way over the top with profanity just to be shocking and not in any appreciable way that is necessary to your character or story.

Obviously, doing business with a broadcast television network is different than film since language is an issue on pretty much all traditional network shows. When it comes to premium cable channels like HBO or Showtime where the use of cuss words is commonplace, you've got license to use whatever you like. If you write something for TV and the language strays a bit north of what is acceptable for that medium, don't worry about it. Notes on that specific issue will be given and there will be a chance for you to do a rewrite. However, keep in mind that if you're writing for a sitcom that airs in prime time, and you use inappropriate language for that genre, time and place, network executives will question your familiarity with a show and your overall experience in dealing with the general restrictions regarding language.

Throughout my lectures, you will often hear me say that it is a far better strategy, in my opinion, to risk stepping over the line and then being asked to pull back, than it is to be too safe and be asked to write an edgier version. We may never know for sure, but I've been told on countless occasions over the years that executives find it a heck of a lot easier to believe that a writer can soften up a script, rather than take it in an edgier direction. For example, in comedy writing, someone capable of writing hard jokes that might cross the line of appropriateness will do so, but they can also tame the language down a bit when necessary. Comedians who use profanity or suggestive language in a nightclub are often asked to change the wording of their jokes to fit their performances on more restrictive late-night TV shows. But if a comedy writer is known for crafting soft jokes, I believe it is assumed that he or she cannot generate hard material, or they probably would.

When it comes to your concern about a script somehow offending a reader at an agency, studio, network or production company,

I wouldn't lose too much sleep about that happening. Readers have seen it all and I doubt very seriously that anything would shock them. If you're writing a gritty cop drama, your characters, whether they're the cops or the bad guys, will be expected to speak in a way that makes sense for them. If your character is a Baptist preacher, it is very unlikely that he would utter the same kind of language spoken by a cop or drug lord, inside or outside his church, unless this particular man of the cloth likes to swear like a sailor during his off hours. Your goal is to keep it sounding real.

I remember when "Scarface" came out, and people felt that the F-word and its derivations were spoken far too often in that movie. The official count is 226 times. But remember, Tony Montana and company were drug lords and career criminals. Is it reasonable to expect them to speak like doctors or lawyers or nursery school teachers? The language in that film was shocking to some viewers, but I think most people in the audience were willing to accept it as being authentic in the context of what was depicted on screen. To me, the proof of this can be found when you watch "Scarface" on a broadcast network that prohibits or limits profanity. There's nothing quite so ridiculous as watching a dubbed version and hearing Tony Montana exclaim, "Go fool yourself, mother fooler!" What does that even mean?

The only time I would suggest that you consider limiting the use of profanity in a feature script is when you are writing a screenplay that, if produced, would be something for the PG-13 crowd. That's when you run into the concept of tonnage. If your script is weighed down with F-bombs, you can forget about a rating that denotes your movie is appropriate for pre-teens. If you cross the line and overpopulate your script with F-words, buyers might very well conclude that a movie based on what you're trying to sell them will only work for the R audience, in which case you have severely limited the number of people who can buy tickets for that type of film. In a world where studios want to make money, that won't help your case.

I've often heard of something referred to as the "One Fuck Rule," which states that you can have one "Fuck" in your script and still receive a PG-13 rating. Two on the other hand, might sink you. If you're writing a pre-teen/early teen comedy script and use four-letter words, drugs, or sex references, be ready for a reality check. At that stage, you need to acknowledge it won't be a PG-13 script.

If heavy duty profanity is crucial to the integrity of your characters, then there is no point in replacing it. When writing your script, there are no hard and fast rules that tell you what language is appropriate. It's your script. It's up to you. You should be true to your story. But if it isn't absolutely necessary, you might want to give a little thought to changing it or tamping it down a bit because it might cost you a sale or at least serious consideration depending on what audience you're looking to reach.

At the earliest stage of the process, if an executive likes your script, they might tell you that they aren't interested in making an R-rated movie when PG-13 is a smarter business decision for them. If that happens, you always have a chance to do a rewrite and remove the offensive language. On the flip side, you may never know why they passed on your movie. They may not tell you why, so just be aware.

The Motion Picture Association and National Association of Theater Owners have very specific rating guidelines set in place which apply to movies. If you're interested in reading them, the film ratings website has a PDF of rules that govern movie ratings. Check them out. http://www.filmratings.com/Content/Downloads/rating_rules.pdf

One last thing about language. If you're hoping to someday work as a writer on a TV show, you need to know right now that your ears will be bombarded with profanity on a daily basis. When a bunch of writers and producers huddle up in a conference room, pitching ideas, breaking stories, crafting outlines, coming up with story beats and dialogue, it's going to be bluer than blue. Non-stop cussing with no limit in sight. If that's going to rub you the wrong way, you're in big trouble.

Some years ago, the Writers' Assistant on "Friends" filed a lawsuit against the network, production entity, executive producers, etc., because she felt that they had created a hostile work environment by permitting and possibly even encouraging the use of profanity in the ordinary course of writing for the show. She alleged that the amount of sexually explicit language used at the office, by writers and producers alike, caused her great discomfort and that it continued even after she made her displeasure known to all. The Superior Court judge ruled against her and didn't even get into the issue of the First Amendment and the rights to free speech. Neither did the Appeals Court. This young lady lost the case by a unanimous vote of 7-0 and in the opinion of the Court, it was stated that the language used in the writers' room was not considered to be unusual when it came to the process used to produce a TV series, nor did the Court feel that the behavior rose to the level of intentional bad acts. So, if you want to write for a sitcom or dramatic series, be warned that it won't sound like any Sunday school you've ever attended. Your options will be to get over it or leave. I can guarantee that they won't change the way they do things for you. In fact, they'll probably tell you to fuck off.

QUESTION FIFTEEN

CONTESTS AND FESTIVALS

For those of us who don't live in Los Angeles and don't have an agent or connections in the industry, would you recommend entering screenplay contests and attending pitch festivals to get some attention?

Oh, boy. I know I'm going to make some enemies by answering this question truthfully, but I wouldn't have a clear conscience going forward if I held back when it comes to giving my honest opinion. Here goes.

No, I don't think you should enter screenplay contests, and no, I don't think you should attend pitch festivals either. Was that clear enough? I know some of you are already angry with me for saying that because you have done one or both of those things, possibly many times, and I know damn well that other screenwriting instructors and magazine writers might very well recommend those types of events.

Please keep in mind: My position on these so-called contests and festivals is simply that there is more to them than meets the eye. Or, perhaps more accurately, less. You need to do your own research about who will be judging your work and who will be hearing your pitch. Don't just trust the colorful poster or lovely online advertisement. I do not have a vested interest in these events, nor do I have an axe to grind with specific organizers or sour grapes about a bad personal experience. I've never had any involvement with contests or festivals. I just have a working knowledge of mathematics and some reliable inside information.

Let's tackle screenplay contests first. Believe it or not, even if no one asked this question, I would've expressed my negative feelings about script competitions. In short, I'm convinced, after 30 years in this business, that they are a total waste of time and money.

I can say, with complete candor, that I've never known of anyone who was successful in converting their experience as an entrant in a screenplay contest into a career as a writer in the industry, successful or otherwise. Does that mean that it has never happened? No, I'm not saying that. I'm just stating that I've never met or even heard of anyone who fits that description. I also don't know of anyone who was able to attract a reputable agent through their participation in a script competition or, more significantly, sell anything to anyone, even if they won a cash prize, an award for being a quarter-finalist, or an honorable mention for making it into the Top 300 scripts in the Action-Adventure category.

I'm sure the publications, companies and individuals that run these events would disagree wholeheartedly, and I wouldn't be surprised if they took nasty shots at me for digging in on this position. I don't blame them for protecting the goose that laid their golden egg. I wouldn't like it either if someone was taking the food out of my mouth or, more accurately, the money off my table. I just know there are plenty of new writers desperate for a chance to grab the brass ring, and wherever they exist, unscrupulous hucksters can't be far behind.

There are dozens of screenplay contests every year, some big and well-known, others small and local. The other day, Dave, a hard-working writer friend from Chicago, sent me a list of nearly 100 of them. They are presented and sponsored by prestigious organizations, magazines, private companies, and a for-profit school or two. Some of them seem so shoddy, I'd be surprised if they weren't headquartered in someone's garage. Many promise a cash payout to their winners, while others guarantee meetings with big, legitimate Hollywood agents and introductions to powerful studio decision makers with fat check books. As my whip smart, cynical Dad used to say, "Where do I sign?"

For the sake of my example, let's pretend a new writer is going to register for the best of the best script contests. He or she won't be alone. After all, this isn't the Second Annual Cottonwood Falls Screenplay Competition & Chili Cook-Off. No, I've selected a very famous contest with an impressive name, and I have it on good authority that it receives far more than 10,000 entries every year, with quite a few writers signing up in multiple categories to increase their odds of winning, and paying an additional fee each time they do. I just hope it's disposable income they're blowing. If this hypothetical event attracts 10,000 competitors, I'll grab my calculator and we'll see how it all adds up.

When all is said and done, script contests typically charge anywhere from $50 to $150 per entry, so let's split the difference and say we paid $100 to get in the game. With 10,000 registrations, the contest has taken in a cool $1,000,000 at the starting line. Nothing to sneeze at.

Now then, most of the competitions say that your script will be analyzed by a minimum of two readers and a maximum of six, so let's stay with the average and propose that each script receives notes from four readers.

Some of the competitions give script notes to their participants for free, while others offer the critiques for yet another additional fee. But let's pretend you will get the notes for free, because we don't want anyone to think the operators are greedy. I'm not suggesting that these script contests are all about the cash, but ask yourself why total strangers are so interested in you selling a movie? Are they just altruistic do-gooders whose mission it is on Earth to help writers? If so, why? Were they agents in a previous life?

For the event organizers to provide four sets of reader notes, they'll obviously need to have several people read each script. Wow, that's a monstrous challenge. If 10,000 scripts are entered, and each script is the recommended 120 pages in length, that means 1,200,000 pages will need to be given some degree of consideration, and at least minimal analysis will have to be performed in order to give valuable notes to writers who will be trusting that priceless feedback. Yes, you read that number correctly. To prevent this contest from being a total scam, in excess of one million pages must be read and critiqued.

Some screenwriting contests feature a two-month period between the entry deadline and the greatly anticipated announcement of the lucky winners, while some make writers suffer through a six month wait. Again, we'll split the difference and use four months for my example. By all means, let's give the contest organizers the benefit of the doubt. Simple division tells me that 2,500 scripts will need to be read every month for four months by at least four readers, because hopeful writers are waiting on the edge of their seats for the notes promised from multiple sources.

If the event organizers hire 10 full-time readers, each one will have to read and write relevant notes on 250 scripts per month, which translates to 8.3 scripts every day if the months average 30 days each, and if the voracious readers work seven days a week. But we don't want our precious readers to burn out and resent the tons of screenplays they are expected to read carefully. Heaven forbid. So, how about we give them one day off per week? That seems reasonable. In that case, every full-time reader will have to process 9.6 scripts per day for four months. Speaking only for myself, I don't know how much time I could devote to each individual script when I must read about 10 a day, every day. Is it fair to a writer that I only spare an hour to read and write meaningful, cohesive notes on a script it took them a year to write—and $100 to enter?

But let's give the readers some credit. Let's assume they can blow through 10 scripts a day and give great insights on every one of them. Absolutely! But, how much are the event organizers going to pay for the incredibly important service their readers provide? If they pay

$20 per script which, based on my research, is the average going rate, then readers will receive a salary of $5,000 per month, which means a reader's total compensation is $20,000 over four months. Hey, not bad! With a staff of 10 readers, event organizers will have to pay out $200,000 for just those salaries alone. Ouch.

The screenplay contest took a big hit having to pay 10 readers, and they only have a paltry $800,000 left in the piggy bank. Of course, there are a few more temporary employees, possibly some short term, leased office space, lots of advertising and marketing, plus other miscellaneous expenses. I don't think it's out of line to take another $200,000 off the top to cover those costs.

At this point, $600,000 remains in the kitty, but what about the winners? Oh, yeah. There are other people to consider. Many times, only the top three to five will receive a cash prize. Other competitions award screenwriting software, books, Skype sessions with a tutor, even stylish hats and t-shirts. I've seen the winner's monetary reward range from $500 to $35,000, so let's meet in the middle and give our contest champion $17,250. Second place gets $7,500, third place is awarded $5,000, and even though it doesn't necessarily go any deeper than that, we'll throw in another $3,000 as random prize money to be divided up among 5 very deserving writers. The total prize pool is $32,750. Please believe me when I say that the overwhelming majority of script contests, perhaps 90% of them, don't give away anywhere near that amount of their hard-earned currency. No way in the world. Look at their ads, and you will see that I'm being obscenely generous with this outlay of cash. Based on what's out there, it wouldn't be uncommon for a script contest to pay all of their winners an aggregate grand total of $5,000.

Subtracting the inflated prize money from the event organizer's big bank roll, they are left with $567,250. But let's not cut it too close. There are bound to be several unexpected costs associated with this kind of massive undertaking. To be sure we cover everything, and because I love round numbers, we'll throw in another $67,250 just for laughs. In the end, when all is said and done, and every conceivable expense is covered, the event organizers walk away with a paltry $500,000.

Yes, my friends. They profit half a million dollars, while nearly all of the writers, the life blood of screenplay contests, receive zip.

When factoring in all of this information, are you still excited about submitting your new script to the next contest? Just think, the advertising and marketing is paid for, so is the office space, the readers are compensated, the miscellaneous expenses are covered, and the winners have received their prizes. Having spent all that money, the Good Samaritan event organizers are left with half a million bucks. Their formula guarantees that 9,992 writers won't get a damn thing, but thank you for entering and being one of the lucky 0.08% to win a cash prize. They should at least make it like a game show from the 1970s, and give everyone who played a case of Rice-A-Roni and Lee Press-On Nails.

Based on the math alone, I hope you can begin to see the origin of my dislike for these events. Money doesn't grow on trees, and would-be screenwriters deserve more for their trouble and investment. There are two more things I need to share about script contests. That is, if you're still even remotely considering them as a means, or shortcut, for breaking into the screenwriting business.

First, give a little thought to who the official readers are and what kind of an expert at in-depth screenplay analysis would be willing to spend an hour breaking down your script for $20. Will it be a writing instructor or a working professional writer? Hell, no. I don't want to hurt anyone's feelings but most contest readers are either writers who are trying to make a living the hard way, or teenagers on summer break looking to make some extra money for gas and an occasional $5 Taco Bell combo.

Not long ago, one of my seminar attendees from Baltimore confided to the class that his girlfriend in high school was hired to read scripts for entry to a contest and that she had absolutely no idea what she was doing or supposed to be looking for. She also admitted to him that she only read a few pages of each script to see if it was interesting. If so, she would continue to read until she could write some basic notes. If not, she would write notes without finishing reading it or really knowing what the screenplay was about or how it turned out in the end. Still anxious to register?

The other thing you need to know, and those of you who have gone the competition route before can attest to this, is that during the contest, entrants receive countless e-mails from the event organizers offering them added services for additional fees. If you manage to get your script into the semi-finals, but then don't make the cut for the quarter-finals, you can expect to receive an e-mail that says you almost made it and that with some private lessons and consultations, you'll probably make it next time around. Of course, there is a price tag for this assistance. You are given the opportunity to buy their books, tapes, DVDs, etc. Anything to get you addicted to their contest circuits and make purchases, all based on the encouragement of judges who swear you will have a better chance of winning next time. Frankly, I find it depressing—and deceptive.

Now that you're sufficiently cheered up, just kidding, we can move on to the new American screenwriter's favorite pastime, the Pitch Festival. I can't help but feel like a group of L.A. guys got together on a rainy day a few years ago and wondered, "There are so many wannabe screenwriters all over the country, so what can we do to make a lot of money off them without having to work or leave the house?" And so, the Pitch Festival concept was born. It's kind of like speed-dating, but with a much better chance of getting screwed.

Pitch Festivals are conducted in Los Angeles, New York, and any other city in the United States, and overseas, where hundreds or thousands of screenwriting hopefuls want to get their shot at the big time. There are one-day pitch events, three-day events, and many levels of participation. Basically, aside from classes, panel discussions on a variety of subjects, and parties, writers pay a heck of a lot of money, in the hundreds of dollars, just for the chance to sit down with a power player from a Hollywood movie studio, TV network, production company or agency. You need to be super prepared to fire off your pitches like a machine gun because you will only be given a few short minutes to convince a buyer or representative that it's time to make a deal on your projects. But don't blink, because the allotted time will pass in a flash.

Here are a few things to keep in mind before you sign up for the Pitch Festival coming to your town, just like a circus, but without the tent. While your main purpose for attending this kind of event is to get someone interested in your screenplays and ideas for movies, the main purpose for event organizers is to make lots of cash.

But it gets even worse. When you're running from one chair to the next, pitching your scripts like your hair is on fire, who do you think is sitting across from you, pretending to listen intently? I know the website has promised that you will have the chance to pitch to an almost endless array of prestigious producers and agents from screenwriting Heaven, but please give it some thought.

If you're outside of L.A., how much would you have to pay a legitimate, successful Hollywood producer or studio executive to travel to your town to hear you pitch? Is there an idea drought in Los Angeles that is so bad, that producers are flying to Denver and Pittsburgh and Birmingham to hear possibly fresh pitches from writers without credits? Would a producer or executive risk their lives to get on a plane to fly thousands of miles, stay in a hotel, miss out on spending time with his or her family, on the off chance that they will strike great movie idea gold—for just a few bucks? I seriously doubt it. In fact, producers who actually produce movies aren't going to give up a free weekend outside the office to sit in a hotel banquet room with a herd of unknown, unrepresented writers who are dying for his or her attention. And even if they felt like escaping for a couple of days, are you really going to sit there and tell me that established showbiz types count on Pitch Festivals to find their next project? Is that how they conduct business, talking to writers for two minutes at a time, hoping that a new writer without experience, credits or an agent will blurt out the next blockbuster before their time expires? Not going to happen.

I can't blame you for thinking I'm full of crap and trying to stomp your dreams into mush, especially if you're someone who has already spent time and money on these events. But try to remember why I'm talking to you about this stuff. Is it because I don't want you to succeed in the toughest industry in the world? No. First, if you know anything about me, you know I go out of my way to help the writers I meet, at every stage of their career. Second, what do I gain by advising writers not to take part in Pitch Festivals? Nothing.

Quick story: About two years ago, I was invited to participate in a full weekend Pitch Festival in L.A. and I turned it down. I was offered a very nice paycheck for two days of my time, during which I would sit in a room with writers whose ideas I was free to ignore and not tell anyone about. I can't preach about my misgivings when it comes to Pitch Festivals, then turn around and profit from them.

I'll close my commentary on Pitch Festivals with this cautionary tale. It won't take more than a few moments of research online to confirm that I'm telling the truth. There are a few articles that chronicle the adventures of writers and producers who served their time on the Pitch Festival circuit. While there are several first-person accounts, one writer in particular wrote about how he served as an unprepared, last minute fill-in for his employer, a producer who committed to attend the Pitch Festival to hear frantic pitches, but who later changed his mind. The producer offered this writer, the producer's low-ranking employee, a few bucks to attend the Pitch Festival in his place and sent him on his way.

To the writers who paid a significant amount of money for the privilege of pitching their scripts and ideas to a real producer, the gentleman in the chair across from them was portrayed as someone who could change their lives. But in reality, he was a random dude from the producer's office with a day off and he had absolutely no clout or authority whatsoever. He admitted, in his article, that he didn't know a good script from an awful one, and that it didn't take long before he glossed over and stopped listening to the pitches coming his way. He went on to admit that it became a regular gig for him on weekends and that he saw the same cast of writers, time and time again, pitching the same stuff over and over, hoping that this next festival might be the charm. He also said that most of the people who were supposed to be producers or executives were really just office assistants or others who were similarly filling in for their bosses.

I know how badly new writers want to be recognized for their work, but I also know there are people out there ready to prey on naivete. There aren't any easy ways to circumvent the process of writing and getting your work to the right people, and you shouldn't have to pay anywhere from $300 to $800 or more to plead your case to someone who isn't even close to being who you thought they were, but instead a person of no consequence who couldn't help you even if you held a gun to their head.

It would be easy for me to stay away from this topic all together and refuse to answer your question, and that might be the politically correct thing to do, but then I wouldn't be doing my job, which is to impart whatever knowledge I have in this arena. I want to see you succeed. I just don't believe this is the way to do it.

If you insist on digging in your heels and ignoring my warning about contests and festivals, I would urge you do something else that might guide your decision about signing up for the next round of competitions. Do a Google search and find the names of the writers who were fortunate enough to win screenplay contests in the past. Be sure to look at a few years, not just one. Then do another Google search and try to find stories in Daily Variety, The Hollywood Reporter or Deadline.com about the big winners. Locate the articles that report on the astounding career developments that transpired immediately after they won the Fourth Annual Fresno Screenplay Contest & Veteran's Day Carnival. Were they snapped up by CAA? Signed as clients before some other major agency could get to them? Unlikely. Did they sell their prize-winning script to Warner Brothers for a million dollars? How about for any price? Even more unlikely. If you do the research, and you don't find the names of those who took the big trophies splashed throughout the trade papers who report on these things, perhaps you will wonder what happened to them—or what didn't happen to them after they won.

Write a great script, and please believe my intentions are good. In the meantime, I'll wait for my inbox to explode from the bombardment of hate mail I'm sure to receive.

QUESTION SIXTEEN

SCRIPT FOR THE MONEY

I've been asked to write a script for someone else. It's their story and I would be working from their notes and outline. They don't want me to change it, just write it. All I would get for it is the fee, half up front, half when I finish. How do I know how much I should charge?

If the only thing you're thinking about right now is the money, then this situation will resolve itself easily enough through the standard negotiation process. Even if you don't have a concrete dollar amount in mind, you better believe the person who is going to hire you to do the work knows exactly how much they are willing to pay you.

If you're a new writer, or haven't announced to the world that you write scripts, then you may not have been approached by someone with this type of offer—yet. There is an almost inexhaustible supply of people out there who have what they believe are fantastic stories, often based on events that allegedly happened to them, but they are quick to admit that they either don't have the talent to write the script themselves or they don't have the time. So, in the interest of bringing their tale to the public, they beg for help from someone who can hopefully do what they can't. In most cases, they don't have a buyer waiting for the screenplay, nor do they know anyone in the industry. Still, they are filled to the brim with belief that their story will sell. The only thing standing between them and a massive windfall is you.

Only you can make their dreams come true. You merely need to settle on a fair price.

Obviously, this is a private transaction, and not something the WGA will be involved in, unless the person who is asking you to write the screenplay is a producer who is a signatory to the WGA agreements. In that case, I doubt he or she would ask you to do the work in such an unprofessional fashion, because they would know they can't engage in business that way. What's more, if they're in the business, why in the world would they be going outside the community to hire a writer without much experience? It seems unlikely and unwise.

If you aren't a WGA member and someone wants to obtain your writing services in exchange for cash, far be it for me to tell you how to respond to their request. I don't want to come between a writer and their next meal. As for how much you should charge, that's simple. Ask for what your time and talent are worth, and don't settle for any amount you will regret accepting later when it turns out to be a lot more work than you thought it would be, or if the person who hired you is a real pain in the ass.

Without knowing the person who will be paying you, I can make an educated guess based on my own life experience and from what I have observed over the last 30 years or so, that he or she will always think there is more work to be done. The final draft will never be done. And if that person isn't an entertainment industry professional, I feel confident in my educated guess that they will, sooner or later, be unbearable to work for. It's hard enough to work for people who know what they're doing and have been to the script-writing rodeo several times in the past. Therefore, whatever deal you make, be sure you can live with yourself from now into perpetuity.

You should also think about a cut-off point for your services. If you accept "X" dollars for a first draft and your boss keeps you working on that first draft for an inordinate amount of time, that isn't fair and probably not what you bargained for. Spell out the terms as clearly as possible, and stick to them. A deal's a deal.

If your name won't appear on the title page, that's probably a good thing. In the 1980s, I knew a few writers who used to bang out low budget action scripts for $35,000 a pop, and always used a pseudonym. They didn't want anyone outside of the straight-to-video company to know that a serious screenwriter such as themselves would ever stoop to writing crappy karate/cop movies that made Jean-Claude Van Damme's films look like "Gone with the Wind."

In fact, a guy I knew in the early 1990s sold scripts like clockwork to the same company every couple of months for mid-five figure fees. Those movies cost an average of $600,000 to make, and he didn't mind being the King of Schlocky Action Films that were usually shot in Thailand or some Central American shithole and always included several people getting their asses kicked. He didn't win any awards, but who could blame him for making a living? Certainly not me. One upside is that he could always pay his bills on time and he took his family on vacation a couple of times a year. While most writers struggled, he flourished. But since he never used his real name, that writer could never tell anyone that he wrote 10 movies that have been produced and released, because his name didn't appear anywhere. He would've looked like a serial liar, plus he would've had to claim the crap he brought to life. I'm not saying that he was ever going to get hired to write a big budget movie for a major studio, but he couldn't claim the writing credit for anything he ever did, so although he had several movies on the shelves in the video rental stores, he was, for all intents and purposes, a writer who had never done anything. Later in life, he told me that he regretted doing things that way. He made decent money in the short run, but his resume remained blank forever.

If you need an infusion of cash to stay afloat and you want the experience of completing a screenplay for hire on a deadline set by an outside force, then go for it. But if there are any indications that the project will turn out to be the hassle of a lifetime, you might want to say no. Again, I'm not privy to anyone else's financial situation, so I can't judge the level of desperation another writer might be feeling. Perhaps the best solution is to consider all of the factors involved and listen to your heart.

QUESTION SEVENTEEN

TALKING TO EXECUTIVES

I've never been in a meeting with a development executive at a movie studio or production company, but I've heard the horror stories about them being rude to writers. Is that true, and if so, what is the best way to approach them?

Very slowly, from the left, with your hands at your sides, and be sure to smile, just don't show teeth. Obviously, I'm kidding. Is that really something you've heard? I've been in the entertainment industry a long time, and I've never really found that to be the case. Studios and networks need writers to stay in business, so how would it help them to be mean to writers? To be perfectly honest, I've found the opposite to be true most of the time. If I've ever encountered an executive that was less than respectful to me during a meeting, it wasn't because of how they spoke to me.

There have been instances where an executive had too many things going on at the same time as my meeting with them, and it probably wasn't an ideal situation to meet with a writer while they were taking multiple phone calls one after the other, or have their colleagues walk in and out of the office while I was in the middle of a pitch and trying to hold the decision maker's attention.

Believe it or not, I once had a meeting with a major studio executive who was playing wireless, electronic drumsticks on his desk while I was pitching and only put them down so he could begin flying a tiny radio-controlled helicopter around his office. Imagine trying to get someone interested in a project while a mini-chopper buzzed around your head and was brought in for several landings on the coffee table in front of you. It happened just that way, believe it or not, but that guy was a clown in general, so his actions only made the meeting a little bit more of a freak show than it already was.

As long as we're talking about meetings, I'll address the topic of how you should speak to studio and network executives. I'm going to reel off a list of things, in no particular order, that you should remember when you're in a meeting.

- Don't tell an executive that you have the absolute greatest idea in the world. If it isn't, and it probably isn't, they will immediately begin to question your credibility – if not your sanity. Pitching is selling, so if you can't substantiate that your product is the best thing ever, you will not make a sale. You will also not make a good impression. Your idea doesn't have to be the best in the world. It does however, need to be solid, well thought out, and marketable. And if you've already written it, which you should, it better be awesome.

- Don't tell an executive that nothing like your idea has ever been done before. Amateurs think that having a totally unique concept is a big plus, but it's actually an even bigger minus. Studios and networks invest millions of dollars in projects they hope will score, and the last thing they want to do is gamble on something that has no track record whatsoever. Why risk a fortune on an experiment when you can put your money into something that is tried and true, similar in some ways to projects someone has produced before, but with novel twists that transform it into something new? Look at it this way. It isn't an accident that so many of the movies and TV shows being made these days are reminiscent of shows and movies you've seen before – if not straight up copies.

- Don't argue too strenuously with an executive. If you push back on their suggestions in a reasonable way, they will respect your commitment to your original project. But if you push it to the point of contentiousness, you are destroying whatever good will you have built up during the meeting. Pick your battles. If you fight with an executive, you won't win, and it's unlikely they'll forget.

- Don't miss out on the chance to make small talk at the beginning or end of the meeting. An executive will want to know what you're like as a human being and not just as a writer. If they're going to be spending time with you on a project, they will want to know if you're easy to get along with, if you have things in common, if you're bright, entertaining, funny, etc. I have established some good relationships with executives over our mutual interests in sports, favorite performances in old movies, restaurants I've recommended, and even through my admiration for the art or furniture in their office. You never know what might create a positive and lasting imprint in their memory.

Keep in mind, studio and network executives are people too. They just happen to have an important job when it comes to the career of a writer, and it is certainly in your best interests to get along with them. Be respectful, be professional, and don't forget to be enthusiastic and passionate about the project you are asking them to be interested in.

One more piece of important advice: If the executive or their assistant offers you a bottle of water or a cup of coffee, take it. There's a great reason for doing this, but I won't go into it now. If you end up attending one of my classes around the country, be sure to ask. The answer will make total sense.

QUESTION EIGHTEEN

WORK FOR FREE

I recently met a movie producer at a film festival in Chicago, and I pitched him the story of one of my screenplays while he was standing at the bar having a beer. He said it sounds really interesting, and then he asked me if I'd be willing to do a rewrite on a script his production company bought a while back. He said the A-list actor who would star in it was already signed up. The producer told me I wouldn't get any credit, but if the movie gets made, he'd pay me for my work. He said this was the standard arrangement, especially since I don't have any credits yet. Should I do it? Is this a good way for me to get my foot in the door?

Oh, Lord. Before I answer your question, here's a question right back at you. How much hard work do you think it's reasonable for a writer to do for a total stranger who's an alleged producer, when he tells you, in advance, that you won't be getting any credit on the project and won't see a dime unless his movie gets made? That's easy. None. Oh, yeah. By the way. It isn't solely up to a producer to decide whether or not a writer can get credit on a rewrite. I have an inkling of a suspicion that the WGA or your lawyer would have something to say about that.

Don't get me wrong, because what I'm about to say might sound like an insult, but it isn't meant to be one. You said you just met this producer, so I'm assuming he's never read anything you've written. And based on that, he's asking you to do a rewrite on a script he allegedly paid money for? For an A-lister to star in? Sounds fishy to me, but I'm not surprised. If someone can get free rewrites from a volunteer who expects nothing in return, why not? I think you should ask yourself what other kind of business operates with this kind of standard arrangement. Would you trust someone with no experience to paint your house or rebuild the transmission on your sports car? I hope not. Would a real contractor or mechanic do it for free? I doubt it. So, if this producer invested the kind of cash necessary to purchase a legitimate script, why risk having an amateur he doesn't know fix it? I don't want to tell you where I was the last time I smelled something this rotten.

There are undoubtedly many industry professionals in L.A. who would advise you to take the job for no credit and no pay, and to dive headfirst at the chance to do whatever that very friendly producer demands merely for the experience and the networking possibilities. You'll be told that this could be the big break you've been praying for and you'd be stupid to turn it down.

It sounds great, and I wouldn't blame you if that answer is music to your ears. But I insist on living in the real world, where things aren't always so rosy. If you had asked me this question in the 1980s, I probably would've told you to accept the offer. But I was younger and dumber then, filled with unbridled enthusiasm and I had not yet learned anything of value about what it takes to be a writer, and more importantly, about how many unscrupulous people are out there, all day, every day, using every gimmick they can think of to take advantage of writers who don't know any better.

Hollywood is full of producers. Some of them are even real producers! Now that I have some serious time in the game, my advice is to get as far away from that alleged producer as possible and to fold up his business card, if he had one, and use it as a toothpick. If you watch TV, you've seen the commercial that sets forth the proposition that anyone can buy 500 beautiful business cards for $9.95, so don't be too impressed. Slick con artists don't need business cards to sucker people into believing they're the real McCoy, especially when new writers are so desperate for help, from anyone, that they will fall for anything – such as being asked to write a movie script for free.

I'm sure you've heard of the fake casting agents in L.A. who hand out business cards to every hot girl they meet, and you can imagine how many of those young ladies are dying for a chance to do anything to get the right audition. It's a disturbingly popular ruse and it's naïve to think that bogus producers don't search high and low for innocent victims. If you're willing to believe that there are fake casting agents trying to lure the pretty young lady from the gas station or pharmacy to their office to take some pictures, then it isn't much of a stretch to also believe that there are fake producers squeezed into every nook and cranny of L.A. looking for innocent, young writers to abuse. It's sad, but I'm fairly certain my last Uber driver was a famous director.

Here's a quick, true story to help you understand how easy it is to mess with the mind of an inexperienced writer. Several years ago, I knew a somewhat talented guy in Los Angeles who wanted to be a writer but who didn't have the stamina or grit required to complete a decent screenplay. To make matters worse, he didn't have any original ideas of his own, so he cooked up a simple scheme to steal material from other writers. Here's how he did it. He placed a small ad in the industry trade papers, the Daily Variety and The Hollywood Reporter, and represented himself as an anonymous, but known, movie producer in search of a script that could hopefully become his next big hit. This counterfeit producer guaranteed that if you mailed a printed copy of your screenplay to the P.O. box listed and he liked it, a deal would be just around the corner. Keep in mind, this was a tiny classified ad.

Ask yourself, is that how legitimate producers look for new scripts? No. They hear about exciting, available screenplays from agents, directors, actors, professional colleagues, etc. They don't spend $20 to run an advertisement and they certainly wouldn't conceal the recognizable name and solid gold reputation they worked so hard to earn.

As silly as it may seem, the guy who ran this scam went to the post office a few times a week, and what do you think he found waiting there? At least four or five scripts a day. Writers were paying a few bucks to print copies of their scripts and mail them to a fake producer, and can you guess what he did with their screenplays? A couple of things. First, he would read them with the fervent hope that he would find at least one story better than anything he already had, so that he could lift it. Second, he would scour the scripts for jokes or clever dialogue that he could plug into his own weak, terminally unfinished screenplays. For an investment of $20 a week, he had writers all over the country essentially working for him, sending him a ton of ideas and pages full of snappy dialogue he could use as his own, for free, without anyone ever catching him in the act.

So, now that you know this, how much work do you want to do for free, for an alleged producer you don't know? I hope I've begun to change your mind about this, if you were even considering it for a split second. I'm not trying to burst anyone's bubble, but it's hard for me to remain silent about an issue like this. Before you agree to taking a job that isn't really a job, take a moment to think it through.

If you fell for something like this in the past, I sincerely hope you won't do it again. And to give you some additional spine, take comfort in the fact that the WGA strictly prohibits producers from asking writers to write anything for free – and every reputable producer is well aware of that rule. Producers who actually function within the industry are forbidden from asking writers to work without pay. Period. So, if a producer, or someone who says they're a producer, tries to lead you down the free work and no credit path, adopt the Nancy Reagan stance and just say no.

If you aren't yet willing to believe me on this point, it's easy to find out exactly how prevalent this type of thing is. Go to the WGA's website and look at the Unfair List they publish and update on a regular basis. You'll find the names of producers who have brazenly ripped off writers in past years. Many of them are serial offenders who don't care what the union thinks, as long as they can get their hard work for free or under the terms of a deal that's about as kosher as bacon-wrapped shrimp. I can only imagine how long the list would be if more writers reported their bad experiences. Don't buy the lie and don't become a statistic. Remember, desperation stinks, fake producers will take advantage of it and real producers can smell it on you a mile away.

QUESTION NINETEEN

SELL THE IDEA

I have a very good idea for a movie, but I don't want to write the script. Can I just sell the idea to a studio?

Allow me a moment to explain why that question is so intriguing to me. When I decided to teach my own screenwriting seminar, I set out to create a unique curriculum that could be presented in just two days, so that people who were busy in school or at work during the week could get a large portion of the education they wanted in one weekend. I worked hard to devise a comprehensive, but fun, lesson plan, and those in attendance traded their time and hard-earned money to quickly learn everything they needed to know about what it takes to be a screenwriter. I've tried, in every way I can, to give people a jump-start to their writing career. Yet, strangely enough, there's always at least one person in attendance who wants me to tell them how to get away with not having to write a script. I know they have their reasons for asking, but come on. You have to admit it's amusing. It's like giving swimming lessons to someone who refuses to get wet.

I'm curious about the reasoning behind your question. Did you come up with an idea you think is fantastic, but you don't want to spend your time on it? Do you think the idea is better than your ability to execute? Is the idea in a genre that you don't care for, so you won't entertain the notion of writing it? Would you rather make a quick buck on a five-minute pitch, and avoid months of hard work? Do you have a much better idea that you would prefer to work on instead? Are you someone with no real interest in the job of screenwriting, but have an idea that you can sell while pursuing your actual career?

If I had to guess, I'd say you're either scared to write a script, fearing that it won't be any good, or you don't want to put much effort into something you think you can't unload on a buyer or into someone else's lap. Basically, take the easy cash and let someone else worry about what to do next. I understand all of these possibilities, but I also know how difficult it would be for me to hand over a great idea to a total stranger. Even if I could profit from it, I know I'd eventually regret my decision.

Something else about the question disturbs me. You have a good idea, but don't want to write it. Hmm. Are good ideas so common to you, and at such a surplus, that you feel comfortable letting one go? Why would a new writer not want to bring their good idea to life and later take the credit for their artistic efforts? It appears you are seeking a nice payday without having to put in any real time or do any serious writing. Perhaps you lack confidence and doubt your own competence when it comes to being able to express yourself in writing, especially in a format that is new to you. Maybe you've heard selling pitches is what the hip kids do. I wish that were true.

If you're a new writer without any produced credits, and without a writing sample that blows the minds of everyone who reads it, I'm not sure how you're going to get to pitch your idea to anyone who matters. It's not as if studio executives have an open-door policy. But, if you somehow find yourself sitting across from someone who controls a studio's or production company's purse strings, how are you going to convince them to shell out a sizeable amount of money for something conceived by a non-writer who may or may not even understand how to tell a cohesive story?

Okay, maybe I'm being too pessimistic. Let's say you use your charm and people skills to talk your way onto the studio lot and into the office of The Man. Let's pretend you pitch your idea perfectly and he faints dead away from the impact of your original idea. There's no way he can pass it up. He has no choice but to own it right now, like today. Let's pretend you have L.A.'s preeminent entertainment attorney on speed dial and she begins negotiating with the studio on your behalf. How much, exactly, is an idea without a script worth – especially when it comes from someone with no track record to speak of?

Before the studio can make use of your idea, they will have to commission someone to write a screenplay. Since you weren't willing to do it, they're going to have to find someone they can trust, someone worthy of the greatest idea of all time. If the studio chief was so bowled over by the concept that he had to buy it, there is no way he's going to hand it over to anyone less than one of the small group of A-list writers in town. Maybe it'll require a million-dollar investment in a script. Man, that's some amazing idea you have. So, how much will the studio cough up for your basic, unscripted idea, knowing that there is a multi-million-dollar development process looming large in the not too distant future?

I keep wondering about the price tag for your unwritten idea. Will you settle for $1,000,000? Yes, I'm sure you would. If I were an Oscar-winning screenwriter who was being paid $1,000,000 to write your script, I'd be pretty pissed off that the person who didn't write it was getting paid the same amount as the person who did. $500,000? For an idea that still needs to be fleshed out? Nope. How about $250,000 and we'll call it a day? Sorry. I don't think so. It might be simpler for me to ask you how much you would need to be paid for your idea, so I can argue against your logic, but that's just silly. If someone did offer to buy your idea, the amount might be insulting, and if you accepted it and the project went on to become a smash hit, you'd never forgive yourself.

There is no way for me to tell you, with any certainty, exactly how much you would get for your idea. Part of the problem is that there is a wholly improbable sequence of events that must occur first, so it's difficult to estimate how a situation like yours would play out. But if you're going to force me to answer, I'll say, "Technically, yes…

but…". Put another way, if I were in Las Vegas and I could place a wager on the likelihood that you could sell your idea to Hollywood without a script, and without any previous credits or experience, I'd bet against it all day, every day. Then I'd get a massage, lay out at the pool, have dinner, and bet against it all night too.

I'm not saying new writers can't be wildly successful, because they can. I'm not saying it's absolutely impossible for someone to sell an idea without a script, because I know it definitely has happened before. I'm not saying you're a bad person for not wanting to write a screenplay based on your own idea, because only you can make that decision, and no one should judge you for it. I am suggesting, however, that you probably won't be happy with the amount of compensation you could get for an idea and that screenwriting, as a career, is something that should be reserved for those who are passionate about writing. Considering the rejection that we writers face, anything less than true passion won't cut it.

Oh, yeah. I almost forgot. Early in my writing career, I also had what I thought was an awesome idea for a movie I had no desire to write. It just wasn't my cup of tea, but I thought it would be a shame to let a good concept go to waste. I was convinced, based on nothing but sheer enthusiasm and an over-inflated sense of my own good taste, that someone else would like it enough to buy it and do it themselves. I was fortunate enough to find someone interested in my story and he wrote me a check. He insisted that we sign formal agreements and we wrapped up the deal in minutes. He walked away with a solid, marketable idea, and I made a whopping $750.00. It's the last time I ever did anything that stupid.

QUESTION TWENTY

MENTOR

I don't like the idea of paying a total stranger to analyze my screenplay, because I can't be sure they're qualified, but I'm also not comfortable sending my script to an agent until I know it's ready. It's too important to take a chance. I've been seeing a lot of ads in screenwriting magazines for mentors who can help me through the process, so how do I even know they're who they say they are and that they're worth the financial investment?

You don't. But the fact that you're voicing concern about trusting a total stranger, whether they're a reader or a mentor, has me breathing a little easier. You've probably spent a significant amount of time and trouble on your script and the last thing you want is to be led astray or hoodwinked by someone whose only interest is to make a few bucks and who couldn't care less about your work, your career, or you as a person.

I don't blame you for being hesitant about sending your script to an unknown reader. If it's a reputable service that's been around for many years, they stand a better chance of being real, but who the heck knows who they're hiring these days? The notes you receive might be extremely valuable, but then again, they could be total garbage. I don't know if I'd want to base my next draft on suggestions from someone who skimmed my script and gave me a brief analysis cobbled together from the kind of generic notes they give everybody.

If you read screenwriting magazines, you should be able to recognize the names of companies that have been advertising for many years. If they have an excellent track record and good user reviews, and that gives you more confidence in them, then good for you. Perhaps you can give them a shot. My question is: how do you discern whether or not their notes are valid? Who will you double check with, another script analysis service? Won't that cost you even more money? The best-case scenario is that you have a connection to a professional screenwriter who can give you their own personal assessment. If so, send them your script, but don't tell them about the notes you've already received from a paid reader. If there is a consensus of opinion, then I'd say you won the lottery. Take their notes to heart, but don't take them as being absolute. Figure out which ones make sense to you and think about how to incorporate those changes.

You're right about your reluctance to not send your script to an agent unless and until it's completely ready. In my seminar, you will hear me say, repeatedly, that you should never send a script to anyone if it isn't the very best you can do. The rule to remember is that people will only read your script once, mostly because they don't even want to read it the first time around. If you can get an agent or manager or studio executive or producer to agree to read it, which means they will hand it off to a reader to judge, don't expect them to ever look at it again unless you already have a deal in place with them. You have one chance at having them peruse your work and if you blow it, they won't want to see an allegedly improved version, especially if the first time around your script was a piece of crap that they might believe is wholly incapable of being rehabilitated.

There's no hurry in getting your script out there. If you spent a year writing it, another week or two won't matter to readers who weren't expecting to see it anyway. Go through it several times, make it as perfect as you can, and then take your shot.

As for mentors, it would be fantastic to find someone credible to be on your side, shepherding you through every step of the screenwriting process. My first thought is that it sounds awfully expensive. I can't even imagine what a working writer would charge for their time. If they have time for one or two students, each for a few hours per week, that tells me they aren't doing too much writing work for themselves. Maybe they are relying heavily on the spare change they pick up by mentoring new writers. I don't know, because I don't know anyone who provides that kind of service. I just can't shake the feeling that a screenwriter who recently sold a script for $500,000 probably doesn't want to spend his or her spare time teaching a newbie how to format their pages.

Perhaps I'm expecting this mentor, whoever he or she is, to talk to their students on a regular basis, to coach them through every stage of writing a script from beating out an outline, to reading their pages whenever they are ready to be seen, to diagnosing problems and giving notes, to reading the revisions, to helping them make contact with agents, producers, etc. If you can get someone to do all that and they are amiable, reputable and affordable, and they believe in you and you believe in them, then it might be okay to give that arrangement a whirl. Again, I honestly wouldn't know how to confirm that they are leading you in the right direction. I guess it boils down to being a leap of faith you need to be willing to take.

There's something about learning remotely that bugs me. If you're in El Paso, and your mentor is in L.A., it just seems weird to me. It's one of the reasons I think my seminars are truly worth a student's time, effort and a minimal outlay of money. I come to your town to teach you what I know to be important for new writers, but I do it face-to-face. One small, finite investment of money for a clearly specified number of hours of instruction. It's impossible for there to be any kind of misunderstanding on either side of the transaction.

If I wanted to learn how to rebuild a transmission, I wouldn't want to do it by correspondence or via Skype. Maybe it's just that I'm mechanically inept. I just bought a new desk for my home office and had to call someone at Staples to assemble it for me. If I can't follow the easy instructions and diagrams for building a piece of office furniture, then learning how to do so over the phone wouldn't work for me. Cooking shows can teach anyone to put simple meals together, but they aren't showing people how to prepare a full year's worth of meals in an hour or two. If your next screenplay will take a year to outline and write, can you really get enough help from a mentor one hour at a time? If so, can you afford to do so?

Everywhere I go, writers tell me that they're getting a healthy percentage of their education from YouTube. Sure, nowadays you can go to YouTube and watch free videos on just about anything. I know people who have learned to change the picture tube inside their old TV this way, saving hundreds of dollars by not having to buy a new TV and risking being caught illegally dumping the old one in the landfill. These are the same people who watched a video to learn how to replace a Roomba motor. They don't want to put the time into vacuuming, but they'll watch a video and employ Do-It-Yourself tactics to fix a robot. It wouldn't work for me, but good for them. In my opinion, and it really is just my opinion, there is something far too artistic and romantic about the craft of screenwriting for it to be properly taught in three-minute segments on YouTube.

A screenwriting mentor who is giving you a guided tour through writing a feature film script should be with you for the long haul. Face it. You can't outline, write and rewrite in a day or two if you can only afford to pay your mentor for an hour here and an hour there. It sounds like a bad deal for you and a great deal for them. They aren't going out on a limb, but you certainly are. The quality of your screenplay might depend on their commitment just as much as your own. The more I consider this scenario, the worse it sounds.

I wish I could give you a more definitive answer on what to do and what not to do, but it isn't possible. Every writer is different and so is every situation. I think back to the olden days of screenwriting when reading services weren't yet available to writers unless it was done in-house at a studio. What did writers do at that time, without those people who advertise in the screenwriting magazines? Probably what I suggested you do, especially since screenwriting magazines didn't exist in that era. The writers back then didn't have much choice, and maybe the fact that you have so many choices isn't a good thing.

Last, regardless of how you decide to proceed when your script is done, the first thing you need to do is write it, so get to work!

QUESTION TWENTY-ONE

SCRIPT LENGTH

I've read and heard that screenplays can never be more than 120 pages and if they are, they are automatically disqualified by the powers that be. When it comes to the total number of pages, what is the longest and the shortest a screenplay can be?

The word "never" is scary to me. If I co-sign on the assertion that a screenplay can never be more than 120 pages in length, and you do a Google search to find that the shooting script for a hit movie from 1996 came in at 122 pages, I'm going to look like an idiot. No, thanks. Let's just say that conventional wisdom dictates that scripts should not exceed 120 pages. That has been the rule for as long as I can remember. I'm sure there have been exceptions, especially when you're dealing with an epic along the lines of "Lawrence of Arabia," but as a new writer I wouldn't suggest you attempt to forge a new standard based on your own feelings regarding script length, and that goes double for when you have no experience to draw on.

There are a few reasons for scripts being limited to 120 pages. If one page of a film's script is equivalent to one minute of screen time, then a 120 page screenplay is a blueprint for a two-hour film. Of course, like I said, there are movies that run more than two hours, but not very many fit that description. The days of the 220 page monster are pretty much gone. Just ask Judah Ben Hur.

The prevailing explanation for the 120 page script is that movie theaters need to turn audiences around ASAP, so that the next group of

$14.00 ticket buyers can grab their $16.00 popcorn and Coke combo and take their seats. The more showings they can squeeze into a day, the more money they can make, with most of their profit coming from $7.00 Milk Duds and $8.00 pretzels. Every time I go to see a film, I can't help but feel that I'm in the wrong business, or at least on the wrong end of it.

Perhaps another reason scripts should not exceed 120 pages is that the attention span of folks these days might not be what it once was. People are more oriented to, and desirous of, instant gratification, and at a much faster pace than in the past. If you're willing to admit to how many times an hour you look at your cell phone, you won't argue the point that we don't have much patience for anything anymore. In fact, I've noticed people going through major anxiety and withdrawals in the darkness of a theater simply because they can't check out Instagram, Snapchat or Facebook while the movie is playing. Gee whiz, can you really not wait for the end credits to roll to find out who posted a picture of their food? I never look at my cell phone during a movie, but I must confess that I do keep it on my lap with the screen facing me, just in case someone important calls or texts.

Whatever the actual reason, movies run less than two hours on average nowadays, and that applies to heavy duty dramas, action films, war movies, the occasional western, etc. Most comedies come in closer to 100 minutes in length and some are as short as 85, although if you dare to hand in a screenplay that is shorter than 105 pages, I'll bet the producers are going to think something is wrong and that you've left out some strong, and necessary, material.

When I teach a class, I urge my students to aim for 105 pages and if they go a little long, they'll still be in the acceptable range. I tell them they can always do some more editing, or go in the other direction and plug in some content they may have left unexplored because they were afraid to run over the limit.

If I can get you to aim for 105 pages and you write an excellent script that's 110 pages, then we'll both be thrilled with the positive result. I just wouldn't go any longer than that. The better your prewriting outline, the better equipped you will be to know how many pages you'll have based on the story work you've already done. I'm completely comfortable with suggesting a target of 105 pages, but it isn't an absolute. On the other hand, if your script is 135 pages long and you swear that it can't possibly be a page shorter, that's an absolute of another kind. Absolute insanity.

QUESTION TWENTY-TWO

SCRIPT DOS AND DONTS

The screenplay I'm working on right now is in the science fiction genre and I'm concerned about being able to adequately describe the bizarre physical appearance of the main characters who are futuristic mutants. My concern also applies to what structures and landscapes will look like on various spacecraft and planets. I've considered hiring an artist to provide some sketches, but only if it's permissible to include illustrations within this type of script. If so, how many?

I'm going to use your question as the on-ramp to several areas that relate to what you should and shouldn't do with your script.

Use Your Words

Your question about illustrations comes up a lot, probably more than you would believe, and not just in conjunction with sci-fi scripts. Writers have wanted to include pictures of what their bad-ass, hero cop looks like, or blueprints that show how a super cool submarine can morph from one configuration to another. I've heard writers say they've sketched beautiful, multicolor caricatures of their main characters and have included them within the pages of a screenplay because they believe no one can completely understand their story if they don't have a sense of who these people really are. The funny part, at least to me, is that those exaggerated cartoons weren't for an animated project!

The prevailing thought is that illustrations, photos, sketches, blueprints, etc., whether black and white or color, don't belong on the pages of a script, and that also applies to the cover. I can understand why some writers want to use them, because they believe the additional artwork will help, but if doing so is something that just isn't done, do you really want to be considered an uninformed amateur or someone who prefers to ignore the rules for no good reason? You're a writer. Please use your creativity to tell a story with words.

Old School Brass Brads

Back in the day, screenplays were printed out, secured in a standardized way with brads, and either mailed, messengered or dropped off by the writer. Now, writers attach a completed script to an e-mail or use a file-sharing site to park their script, and make it available to anyone they've blessed with their password. Today, there's less need for hard copies, which means you won't have to deal with keeping your pages together with brass brads. But if you do, the rule of thumb is to use three-hole punch paper, with two brads, not three, in the top and bottom holes. Don't use skinny brads, or extra-long brads, and don't use anything other than brads for this purpose. No staples, no spiral bindings, nothing fancy. Also, no plastic script covers. Remember, you aren't handing in a high school book report. You're submitting your professionally written screenplay to an agent, manager, production company, network or studio.

Registering Your Script

We all write our scripts with the hope that we will be able to get them into the right hands when we're done. Nobody is obligated to read your script, so if they do, they're doing you a big favor. For that reason, you should never use your script's title page as a billboard to notify the reader that you have paid to register your screenplay with the Writers Guild of America by including the WGA registration number along with your other contact information.

First, it isn't necessary for anyone to know that your script is registered before they read it. That information has no bearing on anything.

Second, and more importantly, putting your WGA registration number on the title page can be interpreted as your way of letting the reader know that you think they are dishonest and untrustworthy and might be planning to steal your script, and that you registered it with the WGA to protect it from theft of intellectual property. If someone accused me of that to my face, I wouldn't want to read their work, would you?

Third, if you've already gone to the trouble and expense to register your screenplay with the WGA, that's fantastic. You've got the temporary protection you desired. Why do you have to shout that to everyone who looks at your title page? If your gut tells you that the person requesting your script is going to steal it, why send it to them?

Also, keep in mind that WGA registration isn't anything more than a way to establish, with certainty, the date that you possessed it and registered it. Nothing more, nothing less. If a dispute arises and someone wants to claim the script is their work, they would have to be able to prove that their date of origin was earlier than yours. Registering your script with the WGA is very inexpensive and it can provide some peace of mind. But remember, WGA registration is only in effect for five years, not forever and a day.

Copyrighting Your Script

If you're a bit more paranoid and aren't satisfied with the limited safety net provided by WGA registration, you can obtain the protection of a U.S. copyright by filing an application with the Library of Congress in Washington, D.C. It's inexpensive to do so, but it takes a few weeks for it to take legal effect. If you sell your screenplay to a studio or production company, you will be required to sign over your copyright to the new owners. I would advise you to wait until your script is in great shape before you register or copyright it. The truth is, you should not be showing your script or sending it around until it's ready, so save your money and only file for protection once.

If you have copyright protection on your script, you still shouldn't include the copyright symbol or the words "Copyright" or "All Rights Reserved" on the title page. If the protection exists, there is no point in stating that fact to the reader. It's irrelevant and actually may scare someone out of wanting to handle your script. I know of one situation where a writer put all the fancy U.S. copyright information on the title page of a script, and when he delivered it to the production company that was interested in reading his script, no one was willing to read it, copy it, or pass it among office staff for fear that it could somehow lead to legal problems. Clearly, that was a major overreaction, but it happened. I'm just glad the script wasn't mine.

Submitting Your Script Without Invitation

New(er) writers are in such a big hurry to get their screenplays to people who might be interested in what they've put together, they tend to be a bit too anxious. They submit their script to anyone and everyone they can think of, whether they wanted it or not. A good policy is to refrain from submitting your script to people who haven't specifically requested it. After all, they weren't expecting to receive it, they aren't going to read it, so why spend your time pacing around your living room, wondering why that producer, executive or agent hasn't called you? Does their silence mean they didn't like it? Maybe, maybe not. Might it mean that they loved it, but they're so busy they haven't had a chance to call you? Perhaps. But if the person you're waiting to hear from never wanted your script to begin with, and hasn't gotten in touch with you after you found a way to get it to them without their invitation or consent, the deafening silence most likely means the new script you agonized over for many months was tossed or deleted.

Drafts

It also isn't necessary or wise to use your title page to make the reader aware that the script they're analyzing is your first draft. I'm not a mind reader, but I have a strong suspicion that the reader might not want to read a new writer's earliest attempt at a screenplay. Yes, I'm sure that some writers will pretend it's a first draft and label it as such, when it's really a polished, subsequent draft, strictly in an attempt to impress the reader with his or her "got it right the first time" script. I think, instead of engaging in these shenanigans, you should devote more time to your script. You should also avoid calling it a second revised draft. It won't earn you any bonus points. Think about it. How will that improve their first impression of you and your screenplay? It won't. While I'm at it, I would also advise against informing a reader that this is your fifth draft, because that's going too far down the road on rewrites. It's conceivable that a cynical reader might wonder what you got right the fifth time around that you missed the first four times. Keep it simple, and just use the title. Make your script great and the reader won't care if it's new, a little dated, or a certified antique.

Addendum Pages

Don't add separate pages to your script that provide character descriptions or other information that you feel is crucial for a reader to have in order to fully understand your story. If it's important, it belongs in the screenplay, not in an addendum. If you're unable to figure out a way to include it, then learn how.

I'll give you a real-life example of how some people try to get away with doing this. I was invited to a meeting in Beverly Hills a few years back, and the producer I was to have lunch with was looking for someone to rewrite a TV pilot he was hoping he could sell to the Showtime network. He was so afraid of someone stealing his idea, he wouldn't give me a copy of the script in advance. No, he insisted that I read it while we sat together in our red leather booth, with him looking over my shoulder. I did so, and it was an average script, but what I noticed immediately was that he attached five typed pages to the front of the script, single-spaced, and they contained extremely detailed information about the main characters.

Instead of reading the extra pages, I asked the producer why he included them. He told me that the only way a reader could really get a clear sense of who these characters were would be to provide a lot more detail before they even look at the script. My response to that explanation was to ask, "If this show gets on the air, and I sure hope it does, are you going to be mailing out a copy of the character descriptions to everyone in America who might watch the show? Because, if not, what good are they?" In other words, if the producer was so worried that I wouldn't understand the characters without the extra information, why would anyone at home get it? The producer nodded, agreed that his strategy was ridiculous, and then asked me for a few suggestions on how he might be able to communicate that information to the reader without the additional pages. I told him that there was one easy way to do it, which was to make sure the pilot was written properly, and that if he did so, there would be sufficient room for character descriptions within the pilot itself. After all, TV writers in town are able to do it all day, every day. The bottom line: if it isn't in your script, it doesn't exist.

Font

This is the easiest and shortest rule: the appropriate font for your script is 12-point Courier. Period. No wiggle room there.

Emphasis Not Needed

Don't use underlines, bold face or all caps, especially in your dialogue. Of course, that rule doesn't apply to the caps or underlines that are required by format. However, if you use these things improperly, all it does is announce to the reader that you don't think he or she is smart enough to get the meaning of what you're writing, and that they need extra help to really understand the point you're trying to convey. It will also broadcast the message that you're a weak writer and you can't effectively communicate your information without resorting to the added emphasis. Later, if you are lucky enough to sell your script, (a) the director will hate the unneeded help, and (b) actors will resent that you feel they're untalented enough to interpret dialogue accurately.

I've witnessed this phenomenon first hand. An A-list actor was so perturbed by dialogue in a script that was in boldface or underlined, he would literally scream those words in rehearsal. You can, and should, use italics to denote the names of books and other actual titles when you are writing your action, but leave the other font options alone.

Default Settings

The pre-set margins on Final Draft, and I'm sure other software, follow the industry standard. Don't cheat by trying to squeeze more onto the page. You aren't fooling anyone. Readers look at hundreds of scripts a year, maybe more. The image of a properly constructed screenplay page is burned into their memory. They will be able to spot someone who is trying to pull a fast one on them. Again, you need the reader to be on your side, or at the very least, neutral. Do you really want to give them a reason to doubt your abilities? Default settings are there for a very good reason. Use them. Rely on them. Be grateful that you are not just starting out as a writer in the 1980s, when I had to type my scripts on an electric Smith-Corona that I used to lug around in a small suitcase. Not only did we have to keep the margins straight manually, but if we made a mistake on the page, we would have to either "X" out the error or type the entire page over again.

I'll share a short story with you about a writer friend of mine whose deadline was fast approaching on a feature film script he sold to a big production entity in the early 1990s. I'll call him Fred. Fred wrote a very broad comedy and the producers were expecting the screenplay to come in at 105 pages. That was the specific page count they wanted. I was in Fred's house when he got the call. The producer wanted the completed script in his hands by five o'clock, which was in about an hour. Fred wasn't ready. His script was only about 85 pages long and he had an hour to come up with the missing 20 pages.

Basically, Fred didn't like the notes he received from the producer, so he didn't take them into consideration when he was doing the rewrite. He went his own way with the script and, as a result, came up 20 pages light. Up against a wall, Fred employed a silly strategy. Rather than requesting more time or being honest enough to admit that his approach was wrong and he hadn't implemented the notes, he simply added extra, unneeded lines between the script elements. If there was supposed to be one line, he'd hit the return key a couple of times, until there were three lines separating the elements. Fred continued to do this throughout the entire script, as fast as he could, and within a few minutes the script count was at 102 pages, even though it was obvious that the pages were short on content.

Fred drove to the producer's office, dropped off the script, and called me when he got home. You may find this hard to believe, but when he handed the script to the producer's assistant, who also functioned as the first reader, she flipped through the pages and said, "Fred, this doesn't look right. You might want to check the settings on your program." Fred delivered the script on time, but not really, plus he looked like an idiot in the process. He ended up asking for more time to make changes, and I seriously doubt he ever tried that scam again.

Housekeeping – Keep It Clean

If you're going to print copies of your script for distribution to interested parties, make sure you use bright, white paper. Remember, you aren't composing invitations to a birthday party. For those who want to get fancy, please keep in mind that white does not mean off-white or cream or pale yellow, unless you want the reader to think your script is from 50 years ago, and even then, don't do it. Plus, keep your script clean. A dirty or crinkled script with bent corners, smudges or a brown stain from the bottom of your coffee mug isn't going to help your image as a serious screenwriter. You don't want the reader to think you rummaged around in the back seat of your car or the garage to find a copy of your script.

Title Page and Script Covers

There's a lot of conflicting information out there about what you're supposed to put on a title page and what you aren't, and you need to know, it's a really big deal. It might be the first thing a reader sees when they receive your script, unless they're one of those readers who turns to the last page first to see how long the script is. Why give a reader, who is probably a total stranger to you, any excuse to begin to develop a bad vibe about the writer or the script?

Don't forget to put the name of your screenplay, your name, the date of the draft, and some contact information on the title page. Contact information is especially important if an agent isn't submitting it for you. Interested parties need to know how to reach you, so it's a good idea to include a phone number and e-mail address. You can also provide a mailing address, but I'm not sure what the recipient will be sending you. Hopefully, not a manila envelope filled with a shredded script!

We all know how difficult it is to get a script into the right hands, and many writers, especially those new to the craft, will put the name of a production company on their title page to add a little extra cache.

I've known writers who simply make up the name of a fake production company and list it on the title page of their script, simply because they believe it makes them sound like they are already a player in the business. This practice is more common than you might imagine. Writers who are yearning for a big break and to be discovered, will resort to all kinds of stupidity to get the attention of executives, agents, readers, etc. While it's easy to understand why they might want to put the name of a production company on their title page even when such a company doesn't exist, think about how quickly a writer can be busted for doing so, and think about what the consequences might be if they're found out.

First, what if the person receiving your script sees the name of the production company on your title page and doesn't recognize it, or they want to know more about the company in question? If they do even a minimal amount of online research and don't find that production company listed anywhere, I think it's safe to assume that the writer's ruse will be discovered. Instant moron.

Second, what if the reader notices the name of the phantom production company on your title page, and it convinces them that your screenplay is already somehow encumbered, meaning that it is involved in some type of contractual situation? I can see where the reader would be led to believe that the script isn't free and clear and that if he or she wants to recommend the script for further consideration, the executives will have to be informed that a production company is already a partner in the project. Just that fact, which is really a mistaken belief based on what is on the title page, might discourage a real company from wanting to become engaged with the writer in question. Do you really want to spend a year of your life writing a great script, only to put yourself out of contention because you decided to include the words "XYZ Productions" on your title page? I highly doubt it.

I'll spend a moment on the topic of script covers. These days, most scripts are passed around electronically and your screenplay will most likely be submitted via e-mail or made available through file-sharing on a website like Dropbox. But if you're going the old school route and are printing out a copy of your script, it isn't necessary for you to put a cardstock cover on it. However, if you decide to put a protective layer over your script, do not use it as an excuse to create a work of art. The cover, if you insist on using one, will be the first thing a reader sees. If it is covered with decorations or illustrations, the screenplay inside might not be taken seriously. Your name and script title also don't belong on the cover. It should be plain, and even white cardstock is fine. If you have an agent, and they're submitting it to various entities around town, and if they are sending out printed copies, they will put a nice, glossy cover with the agency logo on your script. Yet another reason not to bother.

Proper Credit

Make sure you understand how to properly credit yourself on the title page. Many writers, even those who have been at it for a long time, don't actually know the difference between "Written By" and "Screenplay By," and that can lead to some misunderstandings between the writer and the reader, executives, agents, etc.

Basically, "Written By" means you wrote the whole thing, including the underlying story.

"Story By" indicates that you came up with the story, but did not write the script.

"Screen Story By" means the story itself originated someplace else and you adapted it for a screenplay.

"Screenplay By" means you wrote the script, but did not create the story.

The issue of crediting yourself on a title page also extends to writers who work as a team, but many writers aren't sure how to accurately designate their screenwriting partnership. Mostly, writers are confused about the different meanings of the word "and" and the ampersand sign "&" when it comes to linking the names of at least two writers together. The rules are simple enough. If the names of the writers are separated by an ampersand (&), it means the writers are working as a team. If the names are joined by the word "and," it means that each of the writers had their own turn at writing and/or rewriting the script. You might also see a combination of these two versions being used on the title page of a screenplay that was written by one writer at first, but then handed over to a team for the next draft.

That credit would look something like this:

Written By

John Smith

and

Bill Jones & Charlie Adams

It's pretty much self-explanatory if you take a moment to think about it. If you look at enough scripts, you'll see that a lot of writers just use the word "By" in between the name of the screenplay and the writer's name. That's fine, too.

QUESTION TWENTY-THREE

MISC.

I've taken some screenwriting classes, watched a series of webinars and some free videos on YouTube, and I've read all the same books on screenwriting that everyone else in here probably has. The thing is, I feel like there's still information I need to get, but I'm not even sure what questions I'm supposed to be asking, because I don't know what's missing, if that even makes sense. So, what am I missing?

Unfortunately, I can't read your mind, so there's no way that I could possibly know what you've already learned, which means I also can't be sure of what you haven't covered in your previous studies. The best I can do is shotgun a bunch of random topics and miscellaneous facts, and hopefully something will stick.

Representation

If you're a screenwriter, you'll need a good literary agent or manager to help build and guide your career. They'll get your scripts out to interested parties who might be in the market for a screenplay like yours or, if they love your writing but don't like that particular script, who might think you're the right candidate for a freelance script assignment. They'll submit your TV samples, comedy or drama, to showrunners who might be looking to staff their TV shows, if that's an avenue you wish to pursue. They'll help negotiate deals, recommend entertainment attorneys to make sure your contracts are solid, and they'll even give notes on your scripts and help you develop pitches. It will be very difficult to attain any real success without the commitment of a competent and passionate representative.

It isn't easy to get an agent under the best of circumstances. You'll definitely need multiple, strong writing samples to get their attention, but that isn't the only thing to consider. An agent will want to know that you're willing to take criticism, including the notes that come in the form of their suggestions, that you're not opposed to working hard at the bottom of the ladder and won't let up as you climb to the top. A prospective agent will also have to believe that you will follow their advice regarding business decisions, go along with their game plan, and not act like a diva until you've earned that right.

You also need to know that, despite the number of legitimate agencies that exist in L.A., there are thousands of writers who aren't working and who already have agents. Keep that in mind when seeking representation, because an agent who can't get work for the clients already occupying space on his or her roster is a lot less likely to have time for a brand-new writer who needs a decent amount of hand holding when they're just starting out.

One word of caution I can give is that you should never, ever pay for representation. If an agent or manager insists on charging a fee to work with you, then they aren't on the up and up. The very best agencies in town, powerhouses like CAA and WME, don't ask for anything other than the 10% commission they are entitled to collect when they get you work or sell a project. If the big boys will work with you for free until you're earning money, then why would you ever consider paying a schlocky firm or fast-talking agent who hasn't done anything for you except make a promise? Sadly, there are plenty of fake agents and managers in L.A. who make a living by taking advantage of newcomers who don't know any better, so take my warning seriously. The only time you should be paying anything to an agent or manager is when you sell something or get work on a TV series and they deduct their cut.

You don't need to worry about the accounting, because the odds are that your checks will go directly to your agent, who will take their percentage and send you the remaining amount. Agents get 10%, managers get 15%, and that's just the way it is. Negotiating probably won't help you in that regard and there really isn't much point in trying. Attorneys will take 5% if you use one to make your deals. Not all writers need a lawyer to review or draft agreements because their agent can do that for them. You'll find that out when the day comes. Remember: if someone purports to be an agent or manager, but they require you to pay them $1,000 or some other amount for their help, run for the hills, but maybe not the Hollywood Hills. If you check the WGA's website, you will find a long list of agencies that are deemed trustworthy.

Original Ideas, Similar Concepts

On a totally different note, the more you write, the greater the chance you will eventually see something announced in the trades or up on the big screen that is eerily similar to one of your own projects. It happens all the time and it's frustrating if not downright infuriating. If and when that occurs, the best thing to do is take a breath and count to 100. Maybe 1,000. Don't jump the gun and accuse someone of stealing your idea or your script unless you have incontrovertible proof that it actually happened, and you can easily afford to hire a much better attorney than the one who will be brought on to defend the person or studio you claim stole a script from you. Please remember that many seemingly original ideas are going to be similar to other stories in numerous ways, and that you're jumping to conclusions if you believe the only explanation for a project appearing to be a copy of yours is that someone out and out stole your concept. When you have thousands of screenwriters busting their brains every day to come up with new ideas and stories that include the kinds of things we all experience in our real lives or in our fantasies, it isn't too hard to accept that there are going to be thousands of innocent overlaps.

Perhaps you pitched the idea around town, or wrote it up and gave it to several parties to read, and that leads you to believe one of those people are responsible for lifting your concept or telling some third party about it. I'm not saying it isn't possible that someone misappropriated your idea, but chances are it's just a case of great minds thinking alike. There aren't really that many variations of stories out there, and unless you can present unquestionable evidence that one of the people who had access to your project has claimed it as their own, you would be wise to bite your lip and move on. You don't want to go broke trying to win a lawsuit, and you certainly don't want to develop a reputation as someone who is litigious, suspicious, and dangerous to work with.

Here's a true story from about 25 years ago. I've eliminated the names of the parties because getting sued by a major network would ruin my day. In the early 90's, a comedian and actor, someone I know extremely well, was given a holding deal by a prestigious TV production entity. That very good friend was paid $25,000 for one year of exclusivity while the development executives scrambled to come up with a new show for him to star in. My friend was content to sit on the sidelines and wait for someone to create a series for him because he had no ideas of his own.

Back in those days, a lot of stand-up comics were getting deals like that and shows were built around their stage acts. Think Roseanne Barr, Tim Allen, Jerry Seinfeld, etc. As time passed, the production company did its best to find the missing piece of the puzzle, but the parties were running out of patience. The talent was anxious to be on TV for obvious reasons and was expecting to have a show presented to him on a silver platter, while the producers were hoping the talent would help a little with the creative process.

It was a total fluke that I was asked if I had any ideas that might work. I was at a dinner party when I saw my friend meeting with one of the producers and I stopped by their table just to say hello. While I stood there making small talk, the subject of the soon-to-be-expiring deal came up and they expressed their collective disappointment that they weren't able to make it work. Like I said, out of desperation more than anything else, they inquired as to whether I had anything that might fit, and I threw out a simple concept that I came up with previously that I hadn't done anything with, and probably never would have without their prompting. They were interested.

I told my agent what happened and he arranged for me to go to the production company's offices and do my song and dance. I met with the talent and producer a couple of days later and pitched a much more detailed version of the idea. The more I talked, the more they liked it, probably because neither of them wanted the deal to fail. When everyone agreed that we would move forward with that concept and that I would be writing the pilot script, my agent was thrilled. A random encounter at a restaurant had led to a great, and potentially extremely lucrative, situation for me. My agent told me to get to work and that he would iron out the terms of my deal with the producers. I began to flesh out the idea and had another meeting with the producer to discuss development. This time, the talent wasn't there. We talked it through, things were looking good, and I went home to work on it even more. Two more meetings, more writing, but still no contract. No agreement on compensation, how I would continue to be involved, at what level, etc. Then, very unexpectedly, the bottom dropped out. Although significant progress had been made on the outline and script, the time on the original holding deal expired, and the production company did not renew it. It was all over.

With no deal in place for me, I was out on the street. I was paid nothing for my work. My agent told me it wasn't a total loss because my idea and subsequent work with the producer got me in the door at a great company. It would help me with future projects. He painted a very lovely picture, and I was willing to let it go—until I read something in the trades a couple of months later, and it knocked the wind out of me.

That same production company was going forward with a new series that starred another comedian I knew, and although the title of the show was completely different, conceptually it was exactly the same as what I pitched and then wrote for the producers and my good friend. I thought I was hallucinating as I read the description of the show because it was identical to mine. Same characters, same story, same setting, same situations, same everything except for locations. My show started out in New York City with the characters moving to rural Kansas to start a new life, and the show that was soon premiering started in New York City with the characters moving to rural upstate New York's border with Canada to begin their new lives. If there was ever a slam dunk case of having an idea stolen, this had to be it.

Furious, I called my agent, who already knew about the show. He didn't seem to be upset at all and that made me even angrier. It was obvious that I had been ripped off and I wondered why he didn't seem to care. When I told him that I was going to hire a lawyer and go after the production company, he wished me luck and told me not to expect him to testify in court on my behalf. You see, he wanted to be able to work with those producers again, and the network that would be airing the show, and he wasn't about to throw it all away simply because they stole a fairly new writer's idea. He didn't even deny that they were thieves. He admitted that I was right, but it wasn't worth the negative consequences if I accused the producers of doing me dirty. It was immediately apparent that my agent was just thinking of the future, and himself, betting that his relationship with them was a lot more valuable than having me as a client.

He added that, if I went forward with legal action, those producers would never have anything to do with me again, and that the companies they worked with would blackball me as well. He went so far as to rattle off the names of everyone who might be connected to these producers, and the network, and it didn't seem like the list would ever end. So, did I want to fight some of the most powerful TV folks in the business over a small payday, or turn the other cheek and keep building my rapport with them? As mad as I was, and as much as I wanted vindication and recognition for my work, I let bygones be bygones. I never mentioned it to the producers, never complained, and never made waves. The show came and went in short order, and I continued writing. I also fired my agent. The moral of the story is: think hard before you go to war with an enemy that can hurt you a lot more than you can hurt them.

Don't Overwrite

Not everything you can possibly think of belongs on the page. Make your point, then move on. Give your character the words he or she needs to say to convey a message, then move on. Write enough to describe what's happening without leaving anything important out, then move on. Be honest. When you flip through the pages of a script and your eyes are assaulted by an onslaught of massive, black paragraphs of action and description leaving very little white space, is that a script you're dying to read? No. If your script looks like it took an entire toner cartridge to print just one copy, no one will want to look at it, and isn't getting it read the whole reason you wrote it in the first place?

I know this is a gross analogy, but the visualization might help me make a point you'll remember. Think of a screenplay as a partially decomposed body. The skeleton is there and a good deal of the meat remains, but a lot of what made up the person when they were alive is gone. Still, examining the carcass will allow you to form a very accurate impression of what the person looked like. A script has the skeleton of the story there—the backbone that holds it upright. Attached to the skeleton is just enough flesh, action and dialogue, to tell your complete story.

Listen to the way people speak. Do they say everything they have on their minds? Only the annoying ones do. Pay attention to the conversations in movies and you'll be shocked to find that they are a lot shorter than you think and less complete than the exchanges you write. People in real life don't finish every sentence, answer every question, wrap up every encounter with a goodbye, etc.

The same goes for your descriptions. If your hero drives a 1967 Chevy Camaro SS, your reader probably doesn't need to know where the white, bumble bee striping is on that particular model, how much horsepower the engine produces, or what the differences are between the Limited Edition SS and the standard Camaro. Therefore, please don't tell me! Yes, it's a cool, vintage, All American muscle car. I get it. I'm a fan and the details are not lost on me. But if you do that with all the descriptions throughout your screenplay, from locations to characters to action, I'll die of old age before I finish reading it—if I do finish it. In general, include everything that is absolutely vital and get rid of everything else.

QUESTION TWENTY-FOUR

13 COMMANDMENTS

There are times when I write every day, but then I won't do any writing for a few weeks, even months, and I worry about whether or not I have what it takes to be a professional screenwriter. Do you write every day?

No. But there are instructors everywhere who tell their students that "real" screenwriters write at least a minimal amount every day. To me, that sounds like a quota. In other words, a job that requires you to crank out an arbitrary number of pages a day, regardless of your state of mind. I can't imagine that most of the pages that come out of that process will be among the best you've written. Most of my friends in Los Angeles are writers, either in TV or film, and I seriously doubt that any of them write every day. If they did, I'm sure I would've heard them complaining by now. I wonder if a plumber has to snake a certain number of toilets every day to be considered a "real" plumber.

Screenwriting is an art form like any other, and I believe that artists work when they are sufficiently inspired to do so. For example, my sister is a fine artist, and I know that she goes through phases where she works every day, frantically painting the amazing images that occupy her mind. There are also periods when she can't bear to look at a canvas. If there's a deadline involved, I think it's easier to manufacture the urge to create, but in my case, I don't do my best work unless I'm really feeling it.

I don't write every day when I'm doing a script on spec. That doesn't mean I'm not lost in thought about the project, I'm just not sitting at my computer wondering what to write next. Obviously, if I'm on the payroll of a TV show or movie project, you better believe I'm writing every day and probably all day and night, especially if it's for a series. That's the drill. If you aren't in the office by 10:00 a.m. and out at 1:00 a.m. or later, you're slacking off.

Since I'm assuming you're relatively new to screenwriting, I can allay your fears and insecurities somewhat and tell you not to be so hard on yourself if you don't write every day, every week, or every month. There, you're off the hook. I hope you feel better! Instead of being concerned that you don't write every day, you should make sure that, when you do write, you're following a sound strategy that includes outlining. What's more important than writing every day is considering the bigger picture and the overall commitment you will have to make in order to have a career as a writer.

In aid of that goal, I put together a list of my Thirteen Commandments of Screenwriting for new writers to consider. Look at them and see how many, if any, apply to you.

1. If you don't love to write, don't be a writer.
2. If writing feels like a chore you are being forced to do, don't be a writer.
3. If you can't stay in the chair long enough to get your work done, don't be a writer.
4. If your main reason for writing is to make a lot of money, don't be a writer.
5. If you need some type of guarantee that your script will sell, don't be a writer.
6. If you don't like to rewrite or actually believe that your scripts don't require it, don't be a writer.

7. If you don't believe that the standard rules of screenwriting, such as formatting, page count, story structure, etc., apply to you, don't be a writer.

8. If you aren't willing to take constructive criticism, don't be a writer.

9. If you are inflexible about collaborating on a script or accepting notes from a prospective buyer, don't be a writer.

10. If you can't seem to generate an original idea every now and then, don't be a writer.

11. If you have work to do, but aren't willing to make time to write by giving up far less important pursuits, don't be a writer.

12. If you can't take the time to learn how to properly pitch your projects and to practice pitching, don't be a writer.

13. If you've already written a script or two and haven't sold one of them, and this rejection has discouraged you to the point of inaction, don't be a writer.

Look, writing is hard work. It messes with your mind. There is no reason to sugarcoat it. Much of the time you're doing it alone, for long stretches, without feedback or encouragement, and the challenge of breaking into the industry is daunting to say the least. You either have what it takes or you don't. Only you know what's deep inside of you.

Should you decide to pursue a career in writing, you might be happy to know that there are mental health professionals in L.A. who specialize in providing therapy to screenwriters. That's not a joke.

QUESTION TWENTY-FIVE

HOW I GOT STARTED

When did you know you wanted to be a screenwriter, and how did you get started?

I never set out to be a screenwriter. While I've always loved movies and occasionally came up with an original idea for a movie I'd pay to see, I never aspired to be a writer. It was just never my plan. All indications were that I would be some type of attorney, although I used to dream of being the owner of a nightclub like Rick's Café Américain in downtown Casablanca. Then I could wear a white dinner jacket and say something cool like, "We'll always have Paris". As for how I got started, it was an accident, pure and simple. I'll tell you exactly how it all went down, and it won't take long for you to realize that it will mostly likely never happen that way for anyone else.

In some respects, I got lucky. I didn't have to struggle for years, starving, living in a fourth floor walk-up with no hot water, paying my dues, suffering on the periphery of a career, before I showed up on the showbiz radar. But in other ways, I was incredibly ill-prepared to work as a writer, at least at the start. At that time, there were only a few books available on screenwriting and the internet didn't exist, which made finding information a lot tougher. Unless you were studying film at UCLA, USC or AFI, there weren't that many writers in L.A. who were willing to teach new writers how to put together a script and gain a foothold in Hollywood. As a result, my friends and I had to learn the ropes the hard way, mostly on our own.

It may seem admirable, but not knowing anything and without the benefit of having a mentor, it's easy to make a lot of mistakes that can stay with you for years. That's why I encourage anyone who wants to be a writer to get as much education as they can, in any form they can, from as many sources as they can, before they dive in recklessly. If, after reading this book, all you walk away with are my methods for outlining and defeating procrastination, then you'll be a lot further along after an hour or two than I was after my first year.

My rapid journey to becoming a screenwriter commenced when a set of rather unremarkable events, all of which had almost nothing to do with me, converged with a couple of seemingly unrelated occurrences that were sprinkled with more than a few implausible coincidences. It was like winning the lottery, except in my case, I didn't even buy a ticket. It basically fell into my lap.

In 1986, I was living in Los Angeles, about to graduate from law school. My Mom and Dad were ecstatic. My late, older brother Bob, was a stand-up comedian, and my sister Sandy, a fine artist. If our parents were going to be satisfied with having just one kid who succumbed to their pressure and got a real job, it would have to be me.

My only interest in being an attorney revolved around the area of Criminal Defense work. I had the opportunity to witness the inner workings of the system during three internships that had me function as a Certified Law Student permitted to make Court appearances for the District Attorney's Office, a law clerk for the Supervising Judge of the Los Angeles County Superior Courts, and as an assistant to a frighteningly shady Criminal Defense lawyer in Beverly Hills whose clientele consisted mostly of scary, big time cocaine dealers in Southern California who were in cahoots with famous drug lords in Colombia.

What I remember most fondly from that era is that the D.A. I worked with in Santa Monica immediately transferred me to West Los Angeles simply because I didn't think it made sense to waste taxpayer money on prosecuting hookers. The Judge I did research for was hoping I would marry his stepdaughter and get her out of the house, and the Criminal Defense attorney near Rodeo Drive gave me a briefcase full of cash the first time I met him, and asked me to bring it to his office because he was afraid of being carjacked or stopped by the Feds with that much money in the car. Obviously, he wasn't too concerned about the same fate befalling me.

If I were going to practice law, I'd have to pass the California bar exam and get hired by the L.A. District Attorney's Office, the springboard to the world of crime. As I recall, the starting salary was $25,000 a year, and if I were fortunate enough to get the gig, I'd have to find a way to live in Los Angeles on $2,083 a month before taxes. Still, that was the accepted path. The best way to become an effective Criminal Defense lawyer is to start out as a Prosecutor, do that for two or three years, get the hang of it, and then switch sides. That's where the money is, unless you lose an important case, at which time a disappointed gangster puts out a hit on you.

A month or two before graduation, I had a dream. It played out like an amazingly detailed, Cold War spy story. But before I get into the dream, there's something you need to know about me. I'm a movie fanatic. But I don't just watch movies, I eat them, I chew them up, savor them, swallow them, and then digest them. I memorize dialogue as it's playing out in real time. I retain it, along with character names, traits and behaviors, and I will watch the same movie over and over again, analyzing it in a slightly different way during and after each viewing. If I can, I'll find someone to discuss it with, and maybe argue with. It's ridiculous, but true. Movies go in through my eyes and ears, bounce around in my skull like a Super Ball and encircle my heart like a baby blanket, but they never come out. That can be good or bad. While some movies affect me so much in a positive way, some have the opposite effect and I just can't seem to evict them from my mind. But I wouldn't change it. Good movies, mostly from the 1930s through the 1980s, have enriched my life, and pummeled me like cinematic sledgehammers. They affect me deeply.

Most films from more recent days, on the other hand, are like gnats that just tend to annoy me. Over the years, there has been a huge disparity in the overall quality of storytelling. But if I get into that discussion now, I'll never finish this answer.

I'll end my love letter to movies by saying this: One day in November 1969, I asked my Dad for 50 cents so that I could go to the movies. He said no, probably because I didn't do a good enough job raking the leaves in our backyard. We were living in upstate New York and Autumn was the time we dragged damp, rotting leaves into big piles and tried to burn them. It was legal back then. If the wind blew, the leaves would scatter across the street onto the lawns of our neighbors, their leaves would land on ours, and I'd have to start all over again.

We had over 100 trees on our property and it didn't seem like the leaves were ever going to stop falling. My father had every right to expect me to get the job done, but on that day, I had my heart set on seeing a new movie, "Marooned." I didn't know of anyone else who had any interest in it, so I was determined to go alone. My Dad was sure I had homework to do, so that was his second reason for not giving me the price of a ticket. The fact is, I almost always finished my homework at school, but that only prompted my Dad to suggest I do some extra work to get ahead.

Undeterred, I went to the movies anyway, but I was going to have to sneak in, which is something I knew kids did, but I had never possessed the nerve to do myself. I paced in the lobby, waiting for an opportune moment, but it didn't come. I'm sure I looked both nervous and suspicious as hell. With the movie about to start, I pretended to be calling out to my Mom and walked right past the usher who was tearing tickets. I made it all the way to the entrance of the theater and that's when the usher grabbed me by the arm. I was caught. Damn. He was going to call my house. My Dad would have to come pick me up and that ride home was going to suck tremendously.

I knew that my big brother would've laughed at my attempt and more at my failure, and thought my rebelliousness was awesome. My sister would've demanded that I leave her out of it. My Mom would've rebuked me by telling me how the neighbor's boy was going to be more successful than I was and would never do anything like that, and my Dad would've said he was going to discipline me, but probably wouldn't have followed through. He was a softy, but knowing that I disappointed him would break my heart, which was a lot worse.

I quickly apologized to the usher, begging him to let me go without notifying my parents. He asked, "Why did you try to sneak in to see 'Marooned'?" I told him it was because I love movies and I didn't have the money to buy a ticket. Yes, I was that broke. The usher said, "I love movies, too. That's why I work here, so I can see the new ones as soon as they come out." Then he smiled and let me go. Not home, but into the theater. He understood. Unfortunately, "Marooned" wasn't very good. The cast however, was top notch. Gregory Peck, Gene Hackman, Richard Crenna, James Franciscus, David Janssen, Lee Grant, etc. But I got to see it and that's all that mattered on that day.

Back to 1986, and my dream. I like movies about espionage, so a cat and mouse game between agents from the United States and Russia is right up my alley, even if I'm asleep. My dream had a great cast. Clint Eastwood was the CIA agent and Charles Bronson was KGB. The story itself had to do with a Soviet scientist who was being forced to create a nuclear weapon that could be used to dominate the world and how he would use his granddaughter, a famous Russian ballerina, to smuggle the technical specifications to the West while on a goodwill tour of America.

In the meantime, a CIA agent defies orders, takes action on his own that turns out all right in the end, but which risked creating an international incident. As punishment, he is assigned the boring task of keeping tabs on the Soviet dancers as they performed around the U.S.A.

When the Russian ballerina with the plans for the nuclear weapon defects, who do you think she runs to? Clint Eastwood, the disgraced CIA agent. When the Kremlin finds out she is gone and might have stolen their formula for the nukes, who do they send to America to find her? Charles Bronson. We win, they lose, pass the popcorn.

When I woke up, I knew it was a movie I would stand in line to see. I was actually a little depressed at the thought that I couldn't watch that dream again, nor could I show it to anyone else. That's when I decided to write it down.

Law school is no joke. I was attending an accelerated program at Southwestern University which, at the time, was the only ABA accredited law school in the country that made it possible for students to graduate in two years if they were willing to take classes with no time off. I finished in 94 consecutive weeks and it was exhausting, mentally and physically. With my last set of final exams coming up, the last thing I needed was a story to write, but I did it anyway. I sat in class, scribbling notes, filling in the blanks in my dream, while my classmates wrote down everything the professor said. For those days, I was an imposter, a writer masquerading as a law student. I kept at it, day after day, making notes whenever a new idea popped up. Good or bad, I wrote it down. I would figure out what made sense later.

Finally, I was satisfied that I reassembled the parts of the dream I could recall, and made up for what was missing with new information. I had written a complete, complicated story and as I surveyed a map of the Soviet Union to find the name of a city I liked for the location of the scientist's lab, the title of the movie came to me. There's a city in northwestern Russia called Arkhangelsk, and it was perfect. My story would be called "Archangel," named for the city, but also for the Archangel nuclear weapon that would be the second most powerful thing in the Universe after God. It's in the Bible. Look it up.

I was happy with my accomplishment, and the process of thinking through the scenes in my mental movie was infinitely more fun than listening to a law professor drone on about Community Property.

Still, I had no burning desire to talk to anyone about it. The only person I told was my brother, Bob. He lived next door, and we saw plenty of spy and cop movies together. Bob didn't have the greatest attention span and I don't think he heard the whole story. But when the time came, he remembered that I tried to tell him something that included gun fights, car chases, explosions, and a mild sex scene or two. In other words, it was like almost every action film out at the time.

I continued going to classes and one day when I got home, Bob asked if I wanted to go to a taping of "Star Search" that night, because he just found out he was going to be performing as a contestant in the Comedy category. I weighed my options carefully. I could stand in the wings, off stage, as my brother told jokes, or I could stay home and read a few more Labor Law cases. I went to the show.

Bob won that night, and one of the judges, a personal manager named Mike, asked my brother if he was seeking representation. He was. Mike invited my brother to his office for a meeting the following day. Bob was over the moon. Although he was a raunchy comic, he pulled out a win on a squeaky clean TV competition show with major ratings. With that exposure, his career was sure to take off. The problem was that he'd have to do it all again next week and he didn't have another two minutes of clean material.

The next day when I got home from school, Bob was waiting on the front steps. His wife took his car to go grocery shopping and he had no way to get to his meeting with Mike in Century City. I was forced to make another tough choice between drafting a pleading for a mock appellate tribunal and driving Bob to the other side of town in bumper to bumper L.A. traffic. I chose the traffic.

While Bob and Mike talked behind closed doors, I waited uneventfully in the lobby. Suddenly, Bob bounded out and told me that Mike wanted to speak to me. About what? My brother said that he told Mike about "Archangel," and he wanted to hear more.

I entered the office and dove right in to the story. I was totally oblivious to the fact that I was in the act of pitching my movie. Hell,

I didn't even know what pitching was outside of baseball terminology. I couldn't have been more than three minutes into my awkward speech when Mike interrupted and told me that he had a couple of buddies who might be interested in a story like mine. He asked if it would be okay for him to call them and set up a meeting? Sure, why not? I didn't mind sharing the story, but didn't expect anything beyond that.

A couple of days later, I found myself standing in the offices of the Phoenix Entertainment Group on Beverly and San Vicente, the edge of Beverly Hills, ready to verbally present my movie to "The Two Gerrys," producers Gerald Isenberg and Gerald Abrams. Before I go any further, yes, Gerry Abrams has a son by the name of J.J. Abrams.

The Gerrys weren't just two of the nicest guys I've ever had the pleasure of meeting during my time in the entertainment industry, but they were two of the nicest guys I've ever met—period. They teased me a bit at first, asking me what the heck I was doing dreaming up movies when I was supposed to be studying law and making my Jewish ancestors proud. They made it so easy and so comfortable, that "Archangel" poured out of my mouth like melted chocolate.

I was about half way through my pitch and the Gerrys did exactly what Mike did. They stopped me with a question, "Who represents you, Jeff?" Who represents me? Nobody. Why would I need someone to represent me? I'm a law student who was about to start my expensive Bar-Bri California bar exam prep course. They very casually told me they wanted to buy my spy story, but that I would need an agent to look after my best interests. Okay, what the fuck is going on here?

One of the Gerrys called Stu Miller, the head of the literary department at APA, the Agency for the Performing Arts. They gave Stu the shorthand version of events, and sent me over. But before I left the office, the Gerrys asked me if I had a treatment for "Archangel." Yep. That was the right answer and they asked me to drop it off at their office tomorrow. Absolutely, Gerrys.

As I walked out into the L.A. sunshine, I wondered what the hell a treatment was. I agreed to deliver one, so I needed to find out ASAP. I asked around and got some really bad advice. I was told that a treatment was a written version of the story, basically in essay form.

I dropped by APA on my way home, signed a few documents, and had an agent in about two minutes. I then rushed to my apartment and began typing out my story on my electric Smith-Corona. The hours passed and aside from banging on the keys, the only other thing I did was eat a bag of Mexican food from Taco Bell that grew colder, soggier and more disgusting by the minute. I had no time for homework and I knew I would be totally exhausted in class the next day, but I had to get the treatment done. I shot my mouth off about having one already prepared and the Gerrys called my bluff. I finished at about 9:00 a.m. My treatment contained the entire story, some action scenes and dialogue I thought were cool, etc.

I went to school, wore my sunglasses in class so that the professor wouldn't know I was sleeping, and headed over to the Phoenix Entertainment Group as soon as school let out.

The Gerrys didn't want me to just drop off the treatment and run. I think they were entertained by my confused, unpolished approach. Anyway, they wanted to talk to me again. I entered their office and handed them my treatment. It was 45 pages long, double spaced. They looked at each other, then at me, and began to laugh their asses off. One of the Gerrys said, "This isn't a treatment, I don't know what this is." The other Gerry chimed in with, "All we have to do is add a few more lines of dialogue and break up the paragraphs, and the script is done." I wish I could say that was the last time I lied about knowing what I was doing at the beginning of my career. Far from it. Very far.

I received a modest check from the Gerrys, minus APA's 10% and it was official. I was a professional screenwriter, but not really. Two things prevented that from being true. First, I still had to get my Juris Doctor diploma in a couple of weeks and follow it up with a license to practice law, or incur the wrath of Mom and Dad. Second, I didn't have another original idea to sell, nor did I have the slightest notion of how to write a script if I were ever blessed with another worthy dream. I was stuck between two very diverse worlds. One was a drag, the other seemed like fun. In my innocent ignorance, I couldn't understand why people were always complaining about how difficult it is to get into the Hollywood game. I hit pay dirt the first time I picked up a shovel.

I walked at my graduation and took home a gorgeous diploma. I gave it to my folks since they wanted it a lot more than I did. They framed it, found a prominent place for it on a wall in their house in Scottsdale, and regardless of whatever amount of success I've been able to amass as a writer, my Mom spent at least 15 more years introducing me to her friends and total strangers as her son, the lawyer.

I began to study for the bar exam and was miserable. I found a part time job as a Legal Research and Writing instructor at a paralegal school across town. Reviewing law during the day, teaching law at night, I let my mind run free during off hours, hoping I would conjure up another original concept for a movie, but nothing bubbled up in my brain.

My brother Bob had just taped an HBO Young Comedians Special hosted by Rodney Dangerfield, and asked me to spend the weekend with him in Las Vegas. It promised to be a welcome distraction, so I jumped at the chance. Plus, my brother said he'd introduce me to Rodney. I consider myself to be something of a comedy historian, having grown up watching all of the greats on TV and in the Catskills. Rodney was certainly someone I would drive through the desert to see.

On the way out of town, I asked Bob to stop at APA's offices on Sunset Boulevard. I went in and asked to see my agent. Stu had passed me off to someone else because I had no business to transact and the head of the literary department couldn't be expected to waste his valuable time on me. I walked into my new agent's office and asked for advice. What can I do to be more productive? Is there a secret formula for coming up with marketable ideas? He didn't have an answer for me, but he did ask how my bar prep was going. I told him I was taking a pause for the weekend and was heading up to Lost Wages, Nevada to meet Rodney Dangerfield, the comic legend who recently had a huge hit with "Back To School." My agent said, "Wow, what a coincidence, I just got the screenplay for Rodney's next movie messengered to me, and it's here someplace." He fumbled through stacks of scripts on his desk and finally found it. "You want to read it?" I said yes, he handed it to me and I left. That was the moment that would change my life forever. I'm still not sure it was for the better.

On the way to Las Vegas, I read the script. It was the first screenplay I ever held in my hands. The format was interesting, but that was about it. I loved Rodney's stand-up and movies, but this just wasn't his style. It didn't sound like his voice. I took a small piece of paper from my pocket and jotted down a few notes. I didn't have a reason for doing so, but I wanted to remember some parts of the story that didn't make sense to me. After all, I would be writing my own scripts one day and I needed to figure out how.

We arrived on the Strip and headed straight for Caesar's Palace. Walking in, it was impossible to miss Rodney Dangerfield in the casino. He was rolling the dice at a craps table, wearing a bathrobe with images of playing cards on it. Dozens of people were crowded around, asking for autographs and pictures. Rodney begged off and asked his fans to give him a minute to win his money back. When Rodney saw Bob, he stopped what he was doing to say hello. Bob said, "Rodney, this is my brother, Jeff. He came from L.A. to meet you." Rodney shook my hand and invited me to be his guest at his show that night. Not having much of a filter, I said, "Thanks, Rodney. You know, I read the script for your next movie on the way here and I can't believe you're doing it." He asked why and I replied, "It isn't funny." Rodney's face went from a rosy pink to stark white in a split second. Shaken, he said, "After the show, come up to my suite. While I'm having dinner, you tell me why it isn't funny."

The show was unbelievably good. Rodney was like a machine gun, spitting jokes rapid fire. I laughed from start to finish. He sent a bottle of champagne to my center table, the best in the house, with a small note that read, "Don't forget." It made me nervous because I didn't necessarily know what I was talking about. I was relying solely on my personal taste and gut instinct.

I arrived at Rodney's massive suite atop the hotel and he answered the door in yet another bathrobe. There was absolutely no small talk whatsoever. As he sat at the head of the table eating osso buco and drinking a martini, I sat at the other end, voicing my opinion on the script. He wanted specifics, so I took out my notes and ran through them. He didn't argue or comment. He did nothing but listen intently. When I was done, he got up, gave me a piece of hotel stationery and asked me to write down my phone number. He said he'd think about what I said and that I might be hearing from him. That was it. No hanging out, no nothing. I left his room thrilled to have met him and in my heart, I knew I would never talk to him again.

Two weeks passed without a call. I wasn't too depressed over it because I didn't really expect the phone to ring. Rodney had enough vodka during dinner to totally forget our conversation, and I figured he might put his robe in the washing machine without remembering that a tiny slip of paper with my phone number on it was in the pocket.

I continued my work and studying, and one night I came home to find the red light blinking on my answering machine. I tapped the play button and a voice I originally heard on the Ed Sullivan Show said, "Jeff? Rodney. Listen, baby, there's a pre-paid ticket waiting for you at the airport, okay? I want you to come out for the weekend. Let's see if we can stand each other for more than a few hours. This is my travel agent's number, call her, tell her which hotel you want to stay in, and she'll take care of it. Here's my number, okay? See you when you get here. Bye, bye, Jeff." I still have the cassette tape that message was recorded on and in some ways, I still can't believe I got that call.

If I tell you the entire story, the whole day will pass without achieving anything else, so I'll cut to the chase. I only stayed in that hotel, the Park Lane on Central Park South, for one night. Rodney and I got along very well and he moved me into his apartment on East 76th Street and the East River. I lived with him for the rest of that year and it was nuts. Again, I had no experience as a screenwriter and had no clue how to write a script or even approach one, but I was about to get the education of a lifetime.

Before I could work with Rodney on the script I read on the way to Las Vegas, he brought me into a project that he devised with Harold Ramis. I didn't even know that would happen until there was a knock on the door one morning and I answered it to see Harold standing there. Holy shit. In the late 80s, Harold Ramis was well known to everyone who loved comedy. We went into the kitchen and that became headquarters for the script Rodney and I would write with Harold supervising. There I was, suggesting jokes and dialogue to two superstars and they were taking me seriously. Much of what I said went into the screenplay for an animated feature film called "Rover Dangerfield." The WGA strike was in full effect and Rodney only wanted to write something that wasn't under the union's jurisdiction. He wasn't looking for any trouble. We never talked business, meaning only Rodney knew how much I was going to be paid for my work. I didn't complain. The experience was worth a fortune.

Every night at about 3:00 a.m. when Rodney would finally go to sleep, I would go to my bedroom and surreptitiously read the book on screenwriting I bought before I traveled to The Big Apple. During the day, we wrote in long hand on legal pads and I would translate it into script format while my boss slept. He never knew, but I was always scared that he and Harold would catch me. If they suspected that I was a fraud, they never said so.

The process was very smooth running and we completed the first draft in two weeks. That was the good news. The bad news was that Rodney would not be putting my name on the screenplay because he and Harold were the actual creators and besides, Rodney said it was important for me to suffer through my first deal. He didn't want me to get too spoiled. I told him that "Rover Dangerfield" wasn't technically my first deal and informed him about "Archangel." He said, "Okay, then you have to get screwed on your first two deals." I wasn't the least bit upset over it. I was living with a comedy genius and was learning more and more as each minute passed.

Some online resources list me as one of the people responsible for "Rover Dangerfield," but some don't. My students occasionally say that they looked at my credits on IMDB and don't see any mention of "Rover Dangerfield." Yes, I know, I have no control over that. I suppose I could give these students a tour of my garage and show them the successive drafts of the script generated on my old typewriter, or maybe the photographs of Rodney and I over the months working together, or even the Xerox copies of the checks I received and handed over to my accountant. Then again, I don't feel the need to prove anything to anyone. It all occurred just the way I described it. But that wasn't the end of my relationship with Rodney.

After the first script, Rodney wanted to get busy rewriting the screenplay I didn't think was funny. We tore it apart and set out to reassemble it in a way more suitable to Rodney, meaning it would have jokes and dialogue written the way he actually speaks. Rodney had a very distinct rhythm and he liked to start many of his statements with, "I tell ya'…". If you listen to his stand-up act, you'll hear those three words all the time. The original script, as written, couldn't have been written with Rodney in mind. Anyone could play that part. I mean, anyone other than Rodney. We worked on it for a few months, with plenty of dental appointments, dinners, parties, trips up to his house in Connecticut, and some crazy adventures I really shouldn't elaborate on in this forum. If we have a drink together some day, ask me. I'm just not going to put it down on paper.

When Rodney went back to Las Vegas to perform, I went along. But when I wanted to go home to L.A. for a much needed break, specifically to see my girlfriend, who is now my wife, he refused to let me go. Knowing how insecure he was, I believe Rodney was afraid I wouldn't come back, which would cause his next movie project to stall out. Instead, he paid for my girlfriend to fly out and he gave us the keys to his ridiculous mansion in South Westport, where his neighbors were Paul Newman and Robert Ludlum. He gave me his car, had his assistant stock the refrigerator with steaks, lobsters and champagne, and it was a great weekend I'll never forget.

We finally finished the second script and Rodney went back into full speed business mode. I was paid, and as promised, he put my name on the title page next to his. It was official, Rodney was going to legitimize my writing in Hollywood. Then, just as I was making plans to climb the showbiz ladder, he quit the project. Again, I can't go into the details here. Sorry. It was an unfortunate blow up with the studios Fox and Orion, and the executives involved. Rodney was especially furious with the Director, a man who seemed more interested in pleasing the studios by bringing the movie in on budget than making sure the film was good. In the end, the script went up on the shelf, and didn't get dusted off for many years.

Albert Brooks, actor, writer, and one of my favorite comedians, eventually rewrote it for himself, and shot a film called, "The Scout." It was the baseball movie Rodney and I rewrote from the original script, but the Albert Brooks film bore very little resemblance to the version Rodney and I cranked out in his kitchen. Obviously, my name didn't appear on the Albert Brooks project either, not that it should have, but the paychecks for my work with Rodney kept me cruising for quite a while and I now had two screenplays to use as writing samples, which is something I didn't even know I would need.

Returning to L.A. after camping out with Rodney, my agent asked me if I wanted a job on a hit sitcom. I said no, because television was beneath me. You see, I was now a professional screenwriter, and apparently a jerk. Don't worry, when you're a new writer, that kind of arrogance and over-inflated self-image usually get beaten out of you in short order.

Believe it or not, the fact that I had been a writer on "Rover Dangerfield" qualified me to be considered for a Story Editor gig on a popular TV show for kids. Having never seen the show, I accepted the position. The sitcom was "Full House" and my tenure on the show, a mere 13 weeks, provided the financial wherewithal for my girlfriend and I to get married.

That's how I got started as a screenwriter. Now you can understand why I say it won't happen that way for anyone else.

MY CREDITS

A writer's credits are his or her calling card. When you're a working writer, those in the industry learn about you in four very distinct ways. From your agent or manager, writing sample, word of mouth recommendations from industry insiders and by looking at your credits. Here's a partial list of my credits from my career to date.

TELEVISION

Funny You Should Ask (2017)
Entertainment Studios/Syndication
Content Producer

Skee TV (2015-16)
Fuse Network/Language Media
Executive Producer/Head Writer

Peter Turner: Perceptionist (2015-16)
Anonymous Content, Inc.
Co-Creator/Co-Writer*

Office Crashers (2015)
Maverick Productions/All3Media
Creator/Writer*

Sitcom Mom (2014)
ITV Studios America
Co-Creator/Co-Writer*

Number One Son (2014)
IL2M Prods./Foreign (Canada)
Creator/Writer—Pilot*

Girls, Inc. (2013)
Ocean TLV/Foreign (Israel)
Creator/Writer—Pilot

Where's Hunter (2013)
ADA Prods./Foreign (Russia)
Producer/Co-Writer

Meet the In-Laws (2011)
CMT Network/ITV Studios America
Writer/Punch-Up

The Bermuda Projects (2010-11)
Bermuda Government/Foreign (UK)
Creator/Writer

Hollywood House (2010)
Candor Entertainment
Co-Creator/Writer—Pilot*

Dogg After Dark (2009)
MTV Network/The Greif Company
Writer

Coming Up Short (2008)
GRB Productions
Co-Creator/Co-Writer*

Mind of Mencia (2005-07)
Comedy Central Network/Panamort
Supervising Producer/Writer

Untitled Jerry Minor Project (2006)
HBO Network/Simmons-Lathan Prods.
Executive Producer - Pilot

No Strings Attached (2006)
Comedy Central Network/Panamort
Supervising Producer

Last Laugh '05 (2005)
Comedy Central Network/Tenth Planet Prods.
Consulting Producer

Balderdash (2004-05)
NBC TV/The Hatchery Prods.
Writer—130 Episodes

Comic View: Sketch Comedy (2000)
BET Network/Ruby Red Prods.
Consultant

Bob Hope—Laughing with the Presidents (1996)
NBC TV/Hope Enterprises, Inc.
Producer/Co-Writer

Big Man on Campus (1995)
Warner Brothers TV/Calm Down Prods.
Co-Creator/Co-Writer—Pilot*

David Steinberg's Comedy Coast to Coast (1995)
SWP/First Run Syndication (6 One-Hour Specials)
Producer/Writer

The Wayans Brothers (1995)
Warner Brothers TV/Baby Way Prods.
Story Editor

Guilty as Charged (1994)
Showtime Network/Visualize Prods.
Co-Producer

HBO First Look: The Making of Blankman (1994)
HBO Network/Berkeley Prods.
Co-Writer

Bargain Basement Late-Night (1994)
Twentieth TV/Barbour-Langley Prods.
Producer/Writer

In Living Color (1992-93)
Twentieth TV/Ivory Way Prods.
Writer

Doing Time (1992)
Paragon Prods./Foreign (Canada)
Co-Creator/Co-Writer—Pilot*

Full House (1991)
ABC TV/Lorimar Prods.
Story Editor

The Sunday Comics (1991)
FOX TV/Dakota Films, Inc.
Segment Producer/Writer

Hardcore from the Big Apple (1990)
Showtime Network/Murder, Inc.
Co-Writer

Comedy on the Road: Travel Tips (1990)
Showtime Network
Co-Writer

The Reunion: 20 Years In The Making (1988)
Cinemax
Co-Writer

FILM

Hybrids (2015)
Vision Films/HAS III Prods.
Creative Consultant

To See You Again (1999)
DreamWorks/Wendy Finerman Prods.
Screen Story

True Blue (1996)
MGM/UA/Pentagon Pictures, Inc.
Co-Writer

A Low Down Dirty Shame (1995)
Caravan Pictures/Ivory Way Prods.
Writer/Punch-Up

The Scout (1989)
20th Century Fox Films/Orion Pictures
Co-Writer

Rover Dangerfield (1989)
Warner Brothers Pictures/Paperclip Prods.
Co-Writer

Archangel (1986)
Phoenix Entertainment Group
Screen Story

*Denotes Development

RADIO

The Roger Lodge Show (2004)
Sporting News Radio/L.A.
Executive Producer/Head Writer

Sinbad and Friends (2001)
Clear Channel Radio/L.A.
Executive Producer/Head Writer

The George Lopez Mega Show (2000)
Clear Channel Radio/L.A.
Executive Producer/Head Writer

The Ed Lover and Dr. Dre Show (1999)
AMFM Radio/L.A.
Executive Producer/Head Writer

Big Boy's Neighborhood (1998)
Emmis Communications/L.A.
Head Writer

Writers bust their butts to get jobs and, eventually, some recognition. I'm no exception. Every one of my credits listed above is 100% legitimate and I earned every single one of them, often joyously, but sometimes one very trying minute at a time.

Not to beat a dead horse, since there is a separate question and answer on this issue, but there are some online sites that purport to shine a spotlight on your accomplishments and claim to be the absolute best resource for verifying credits. It is important for you to understand a key truth about these sites.

IMDB is free for non-commercial use and claims to be the leading resource for checking credits, as long as you're willing to sign up for the paid "Pro" version for only $150.00 per year.

Another site, Staff Me Up, claims to be the #1 site for industry networking and up-to-date credit info. While I can't confirm the validity of their statements, I can tell you, for a fact, that the information they have listed for me is erroneous. If people are really looking to network with me or consider me for a script assignment based on the credits listed on the Staff Me up site, they are in for a surprise.

When I review both IMDB and Staff Me Up, I get frustrated. Neither is anywhere near complete. Neither accurately reflects my credits, and in one case there is a credit entry that is just completely off the charts wrong. Earlier today, I learned that Staff Me Up lists me as an Executive Producer on an ABC Network show called "Bachelor Pad." I wish that were true, because I would've loved to receive EP checks every couple of weeks. The point is, I've never worked on that show. Not only do entertainment industry websites list me as a Writer and/or Producer on projects I've never been associated with, but others, like IMDB, are missing the majority of my credits and despite repeated efforts, they have not updated my information.

If you're going to trust someone to be your teacher or mentor, I would urge you to do your homework when it comes to checking their pedigree. If the best websites can routinely get credits wrong or fail to report them accurately, then you'll have to do some more in-depth detective work on your own to find out who you're actually working with on your important projects.

Take, for example, a screenwriting instructor I will refer to only as Jane Smith. I've never met Jane, but her nicely designed website provides an exhaustive list of her purported credits. Since we both teach classes and our paths are bound to cross at some juncture, I thought it best to become acquainted with Jane's work.

When none of Jane's projects rang a bell, I decided to check sites other than her own. Thankfully, the credits on Jane's website provide not just the name of the movie she allegedly wrote and/or produced, but also the names of other producers involved and even the name of the director responsible for each film or made-for-TV movie. With that goldmine of information at my fingertips, I was able to check IMDB, the online archives of The Hollywood Reporter and Daily Variety and a few other sources that stockpile just about every relevant fact and figure related to films and made-for-TV movies. It's amazing how much information is available, for free, with a minimum of keystrokes.

Believe it or not, none of Jane's projects exist in any form whatsoever. Apparently, none of them panned out. Not a single one. Movies with those titles were never produced. Cross-referencing, I was able to determine, without a doubt, that the other producers and directors listed in her credits never worked on movies of any kind with those titles. Either I was losing my mind or Jane was making things up wholesale in an effort to inflate her resume. One last adventure on the worldwide web revealed that Jane Smith, bless her heart, had never actually written or produced anything mentioned on her website or anywhere else for that matter.

If you want to know how this kind of thing can happen, I'll give you my best, educated guess. It took some imagination, but here is what I came up with. Jane Smith, like so many other writers without any legitimate credits, have to get creative in order to build a career on paper. The easiest way to do that is to count every meeting you ever had as a writer or someone else in the room during such meetings. Let's pretend Jane, or maybe someone she worked for, had a pitch meeting with Studio Executive X. Jane was present when her boss told Studio Executive X about a movie she wrote and/or wants to produce called "Fake Movie" and he said he loved it. She mentioned the name of a director she thought would be good for the project and Studio Executive X agreed. Voila! There's one movie credit down, twenty to go. Jane considers the meeting she attended, with no promise of a deal mentioned, to be a credit. The movie isn't being purchased or made, Jane didn't write it, but she claims it as a completed transaction. Jane then lists the name of the studio she visited, along with the name of the director her boss mentioned. What other reasonable explanation can Jane give for listing movies that were never made and that were never even in development as produced credits? When you come up with an answer that makes the slightest amount of sense, please let me know. Perhaps Jane had some of these meetings on her own, without her boss. Still, receiving a positive response doesn't give rise to a credit unless and until something more happens after that. Was an offer made, and if so, was a contract negotiated and signed? Was a script generated, by Jane or someone else? Was production a go? Was a director hired? If not, how does this social transaction become a credit?

There's an old Chinese proverb that says, "If you make an ass of yourself, there will always be someone willing to ride you." I believe it applies to this topic. If a fake writer like Jane is out there teaching classes, it's your responsibility to investigate and sniff out the fraud all by yourself. If you don't, you might end up paying hundreds of dollars for lessons that aren't even worth hundreds of pennies.

BONUS ONE

OUTLINING

How long and how detailed should my outline be before I start to write my screenplay?

This is always one of my favorite questions, because it's like an engraved invitation to teach my own method of outlining to a new audience. It never fails to come up during my seminars and Q&As and I interpret that as a good sign. Writers everywhere, at all levels of experience, are in search of a reliable way to build an all-encompassing outline before they start writing a new script. This will take a little while to explain, so sit back and relax. But believe me when I say that once you understand it and begin using this system to outline new screenplays, you'll be glad you asked—and listened.

If you're hell bent against working from a perfected outline, I will say this: You're making a big, foolish mistake. In my opinion, that kind of attitude will inevitably lead to a terrible script, that is if you manage to finish at all. The fact is, most writers I've met who refuse to outline properly end up bailing out of the project somewhere around Page 55 of their screenplay. That's where they become hopelessly lost, and the only Plan B they have in place is to surrender to frustration, stop writing in circles, admit defeat, and just quit.

My way of creating an outline consists of several steps which may seem time consuming, but will ultimately save you loads of valuable time during the writing phase. If you follow my instructions, my simple method will help you to fully organize your thoughts. Then, if you have the discipline and willpower to stay true to a completed outline, that outline will, by design, keep you focused and on track and much less enticed to go off on counterproductive tangents from which there is no return. Even better, my strategy can be fun and it will force you to you ask yourself a myriad of questions you hadn't yet contemplated about your story, characters, set ups, pay offs, etc. Once you have answers, you can use them to construct a bulletproof foundation upon which to build your script with nothing left to chance.

Before I go any further, I must add that this is my personal approach to outlining. It works for me, and I've never had any complaints from the thousands of writers I've shared this technique with over the last several years. Quite the contrary. Writers have told me that my method has saved them a lot of time, trouble and heartache, and that their finished scripts are much stronger in that they directly reflect the amount of pre-writing preparation that went in to the creative process. It gives me great satisfaction every time I hear that. Writers have it hard enough as it is.

Aside from reading some books when I was starting out as a writer in the late 1980s, I never found anyone willing to take the time to teach me how to produce an in-depth outline, certainly not this way, and the process I'm about to describe is something I originally put together for myself. I learned the hard way, as many writers do, that attempting to write a respectable screenplay without a real outline is insane, and nothing good will come of it. I often tell my students that writing without a real outline is like seeing a bear trap on the trail ahead of you and diving headfirst into its jaws. You knew it was there, you could've easily walked around it and remained unharmed, but for some unknown reason, getting decapitated sure seemed like a good idea at the time.

There's a second reason for me to claim, for the record, that my method of outlining is unique to me. Recently I've noticed that a few resources for screenwriters, both free online and in textbook form, have begun teaching something similar, down to the most minute details. By no means am I suggesting that these other folks misappropriated my method. What I am saying, however, is that I certainly didn't copy their approach to outlining either, and I can promise my students that I absolutely, positively, did not borrow this system from anyone else. The last thing I want is for someone to accuse me of padding my screenwriting course by pilfering someone else's work. It just isn't something I would ever do. Then again, teaching my outlining method around the country does provide ample opportunity for someone to take more than a pedestrian liking to it. The good news is this: I'm quite sure that if my outlining method helps you with your writing, you won't care who or where it came from. I just want to be up front and say that I'm proud of my outlining system, and it took me years of experimentation to formulate something that I believe will work for every writer.

To me, there is nothing more important than having an incredibly well-developed and detailed outline. Of course, the original idea for your script is the basis for the overall project, and that is something only you can formulate. But without a great outline, the idea won't matter. Without a great outline, your finished script, if you do finish it, will most likely be a jumbled mess that bears little resemblance to the concept you began with. When traveling to a location you've never visited before, without the aid of an accurate road map or navigation system, you don't have much chance of reaching your final destination, and that's exactly how an outline should function in the screenwriting process.

Trust me, many people don't outline at all. A writer will plop down in his or her chair and start typing with few, if any, notes to refer to along the way. Believing that they've fashioned a master plan, albeit unwritten, they move forward with reckless abandon, incredibly confident that they'll remember exactly how their story lays out. What could possibly go wrong?

Still other writers are satisfied with a skeleton outline. For each of the three Acts, they list a few significant scenes, and perhaps some story beats or random character revelations. But if you asked them to lead you through their entire script from beginning to end, they wouldn't be able to do so.

These writers seem to be okay with generally knowing what they want to write in the broadest of terms and are content that they can flesh it out as they go. I've seen many people attempt this task, but I've never seen the finished product pan out as anything more than a stream of consciousness screenplay that may as well have been written with a shotgun that sprays words across a wide range, hoping to hit the target.

Now then, let's get into my way of outlining. It consists of 8 easy to understand steps and it won't take long for you to realize that it's the smartest way to prepare for writing a script that is important to you.

Assuming you already have an idea that you're excited about and that you've been toying with for some time, the first thing you'll need to do is buy index cards. I know what some people will say. There's no need for that because my screenwriting software already has an index card feature! Yes, I know. It's awesome. You can still use it. But I truly believe that the tactile experience of grasping index cards in your hands, and looking at them up on the wall, on the floor, or on your desk, provides a powerful subconscious benefit. Writing on index cards, having the sensation of holding them, manually rearranging them, etc., gives writers a feeling of being productive. There's a sense that real work is happening, and that alone is constructive reinforcement. Don't fight it.

STEP 1: When I'm creating a new outline, I will pick up at least 400 index cards at the store. I suggest that you use a larger size, preferably 4"x6" or 5"x7", and it is mandatory that they be a mix of plain white and multi-colored cards. Buy plain white cards in one package, and a few packages combining blue, green, yellow, red/pink, and purple cards. You'll also need a few black Sharpie markers. If you're going to put cards up on the wall, which I always recommend, you'll need pushpins or double-sided tape. Your total investment should be no more than $25.00.

STEP 2: Assign a color to each of the categories the cards will represent. Using my method, blue cards will be used to describe your main characters and will include vital information such as their name, age, background, physical characteristics, plus anything else that's important for you to know about them at a glance. If you have more character information than will fit on one blue card, that's good. Just use a second blue card to finish out those thoughts.

Green cards signify a single scene or series of scenes that I would describe as having "up" energy. A green card can denote a good thing that is happening in the story, a happy exchange between characters, a positive change, etc. Is a main character leaving an office having just landed a big job? Green card. Is a blind date going extremely well? Green card. Is the banter at a poker game particularly funny and causing laughter? Green card. These are beats or scenes that exist above the neutral baseline of your story. Basically, all stories have peaks and valleys, and green cards let the writer know that what they are about to write when they see a green card is a scene that takes place on the upswing, or in an area of the story or interplay between characters that is upbeat.

Red/Pink cards function in the exact opposite way. They signal to the writer that something bad, sad, negative, or dangerous is occurring. These moments exist on the way down toward the baseline, below it, or in a place that's already in a valley. An argument between spouses that feels like an emotional kick to the stomach necessitates a red card. The news of the death of a friend is a red card. Being threatened by your boss is an appropriate moment for a red card.

Yellow cards are for big, energetic action scenes. Shoot-outs or car chases or fight scenes would be marked with yellow cards. Although it doesn't exude the same kind of energy as a chase or gun battle, a prom with choreographed dancing, high energy, hijinks, an awards ceremony, etc., could also be marked with a yellow card.

Purple cards are reserved for specific dialogue, jokes, crucial exchanges between characters, speeches, etc. Just write the exact words you know you want spoken by someone at that very moment in the script on a purple card. It will be easy to locate during the actual writing.

White cards should be used for literally everything else, meaning most of your scene cards will be white.

Try to imagine what your wall will look like when you have three hundred white and multi-colored index cards tacked or taped up in a grid, arranged in the order of your script's scenes. If you do what I'm suggesting, and you use the green, red/pink, and yellow cards properly, it will be possible for you to stand back and actually see the flow of the script. The ups, downs, and big action scenes will be easy to spot, and if your script, as outlined, looks like it will be comprised mostly of a bunch of down moments (you'll see a bunch of red/pink cards in a row) without any relief provided by up moments (green cards), you'll see it as plain as day and will realize something is wrong. What a great visual tool to help you know if your story is a roller coaster ride or a low energy bore.

STEP 3: Now that you know what the colors mean, sit down and write out as many cards as you can, either off the top of your head or from whatever written story notes you have already generated. They can be in any category and there is no need for them to be in any kind of order at this stage.

Put whatever you know about your main characters on blue cards. If you have ideas for some great action sequences, a short explanation of each one should be written on a yellow card. If you know there will be a very sad scene between two lovers who are breaking up, indicate that on a red card. If there's a scene that includes a happy occasion, like the birth of a baby, securing a job, etc., it belongs on a green card.

If you have a great idea for some words your main character should utter at a crucial moment in the story, write it out on a purple card.

Keep writing bullet points or long-hand notes on different cards until you exhaust all the information you have previously compiled for your story. At this point in the process, it won't matter if you have twenty cards or one hundred cards filled in. The number will serve to tell you how much work you've done to map out your story, and how much work remains to be accomplished.

STEP 4: This part should only take about five minutes. Take a few white cards and your Sharpie and write, in big letters, the names of the major benchmarks that are important in every Three Act screenplay. These are your main headings. For example, cards should say things like "Fade In: Beginning of Act One," "End of Act One," "Mid Act Two," "All Is Lost," "Beginning of Act Three," "Resurrection," etc. If you find that it helps you to know where Page 10 is in the outline because you want to be sure to accomplish certain things in your script by then, make up a "Page 10" card.

Once you've made these cards, and there shouldn't be more than 10 or 12 of them, tack them up on a wall in a long horizontal line that represents the time continuum along which your story plays out. There are some people who won't want pushpin holes in the wall, and for those writers, they can either use some kind of tape that won't do damage or just find a big open space on the floor, perhaps in a guest room or garage, and lay the cards down in the order that the benchmarks appear in your screenplay structure. This will be the basic backbone of your script.

STEP 5: Take the cards you've filled in with story information and place them where they belong in relation to the main heading cards. For example, if you have a yellow card for a chase scene you are envisioning for a time in your story just before the middle of Act Two, stick that card in the space immediately in front of your white

"Mid Act Two" benchmark card. If a green card describes the big moment when your main character starts his mission and this will happen at the end of Act One, take a pushpin and put that card in the space where it belongs, which is immediately before the "Act Two" card. If you know what you want to happen at the Page 10 mark, place the card you've created for that particular story point and pin it in its proper position on the wall. If you know the exact place in the story you need to introduce a character, put that blue card exactly where it belongs. You can also have white cards that tell you where specific subplots begin and end, and if you stick them where they belong right now, you won't be confused later during the writing process. The same goes for all your cards of every color and category.

It isn't difficult to get these cards in order, and you can move them around as many times as necessary. Very often, writers come up with new ideas or they improve upon ideas, simply by virtue of seeing how the cards are arranged and how the story flows in its current state. It's better to make those changes now and to be sure they make sense before you begin writing. As you can probably see, each step of this outlining process keeps you thinking about every aspect of your story and it spurs you to continue developing more information.

Now that everything you know about your story is up on the wall or spread out across the floor, something should become readily apparent. Namely, many pieces of information you need at your fingertips in order to write a cohesive, properly structured screenplay are missing. Where are they? Nowhere, because you haven't spent enough time working on your project. Hopefully you will notice, just by surveying your cards, that there are gaping holes where there was supposed to be solid information upon which to build your script. At that point, you'll breathe a sigh of relief that you didn't just sit down and start typing away before completing a real outline. Don't you feel better already?

STEP 6: The challenge now is to fill in all the blanks in your outline, meaning that you will have to think of everything that's absent from your storyline and plug it in to your index card collection. It might help if you envision the time continuum as a rod that you have in your closet. The clothes you already own hang from that rod, but as you add new pieces to your wardrobe, all you have to do is push the clothes to the side and make room for new hangers. Each time you create a new card, find the proper place for it along the continuum and just push the previous card to one side or the other, depending on what you've decided will happen first in your story.

You should spend your time thinking about your story for as long as it takes, and don't rush it. Each new card can take you minutes, hours, days, or even weeks to create. At this point, you have the freedom to let your mind run wild and free, uncensored, knowing that you don't have to come up with your story information in a linear fashion. If you suddenly think of a cool action scene that could happen near the end of Act Two, write it on a yellow card and pop it up on the wall where you feel it belongs, at least for now. If you think of a hilarious joke for a character to deliver, write it on a purple card and place it in the appropriate spot. But if you just have a stray joke and don't know where it belongs yet, you should still write it on a purple card and stick it in a temporary space. Forcing yourself to come up with new information in the order of use will only stifle your creativity. Simply keep going until you're able to fully bridge the gaps between cards that already exist.

The good news is that many of these cards can be and will be rearranged countless times. No harm in changing your mind during this phase. If you include an index card that, for some reason, becomes irrelevant at some point, get rid of it. If it makes sense to put it back in later, write a new card for it.

Remember that right now, your job is to keep writing new cards, dozens of them, and to place them where they belong along your story's continuum. If you're able to do this in one sitting, as in a few hours, I would venture a guess that you aren't going deep enough. It isn't realistic to believe that you will come up with every conceivable piece of information that you will need in order to write a 110 page screenplay in short order. Give yourself a chance to delve into your story, your characters, etc. Again, no hurry. It's far better to spend days or even weeks perfecting your new outline, and it'll make the writing process much easier and a lot more fun.

Many writers have told me that they came up with some of their best ideas while outlining this way and that if they had begun writing even a day earlier, those ideas would not have occurred to them. Once you begin to use my method, you will probably find that to be true.

Only you will know when you're done making up cards and filling in the blanks. I've worked with several writers who thought for sure that their index card outline was complete and that they were ready to write, only to find out that they skipped a few vital areas. I would stand next to them at the wall and listen intently as they introduced me to their characters and walked me through their entire story. Invariably, I'd interrupt the presentation with nothing more than a customary question, which would turn out to be anything but easy to answer. Watching the writer's mouth drop open is always entertaining and it means just one thing: I poked a hole in their outline and asked them for a piece of crucial information they hadn't yet contemplated.

The first thing to do in that case is to quickly write up a white card with that question and pin it to the blank space that needs to be filled in with an answer. Next, the writer will have to reassess their outline and think about whether it requires even more thought across the board. Keep in mind that you will need to know if the answer to the question will affect the characters or events later in the script.

If you haven't introduced all your characters on different cards, then you aren't done. If you don't have every location and the important facts about them planned out on cards, then you aren't done. If you don't have all the highs, lows, obstacles, action scenes, etc. on cards and in the right order, then you aren't done.

I can't stress this enough: this is the time to do the really hard work. Do not race toward the writing phase. It's easier to rewrite index cards than 60 pages of a script. When you are finally satisfied that you have considered every possible moment in your story and know everything there is to know, backwards and forwards, it's time to move on.

STEP 7: At this stage in the outlining process, the writer will have worked on his or her cards long enough to know if anything is still missing. Their story has been examined over and over from every angle, and if the writer is sure he or she is done with writing up cards then it's time to formally commit to the outline.

All you need to do now is number the cards in the upper right corner. There is no magic to the total number of cards you have at this point, although if your master outline is comprised of 50 cards, I'd be somewhat skeptical that it can possibly contain everything you need. On the other hand, if you have 1,000 cards, you have almost assuredly gone overboard. Typically, my outlines come in at around 300 cards, and aside from blue character cards, I tend to utilize each of my cards for just one distinct thought. Once your cards are numbered in order, you are ready to write. The process might sound cumbersome, but I promise it isn't. I honestly find it to be fun and a great way to stimulate creative thought, especially in areas that you've gone over many times and were sure had been mined to death.

I do have one serious caveat, so please pay attention, because if you choose to ignore this warning, you might very well undo your entire outline and that would be a disaster. Remember, I said that you should not number your cards until you were 100% confident about the order they are in. If that's the case, then there is no reason for that order to change now or at some later time. Have some faith in yourself. If you've spent a decent amount of time and energy on your outline, second guessing yourself now would be destructive to the process. Recognize anxiety and resist the little voice in your head that is telling you that your outline is garbage and you're making a big mistake by relying on it. Actually, the big mistake would be to change it now. Get busy writing your first draft and remember you can always go back and do a rewrite. In fact, it's mandatory to do so. It's called a first draft for a reason.

What happens if you have begun writing, and find yourself still coming up with all kinds of good, but relatively small ideas that will improve your story, but will neither change the continuum of the story line, nor the order of the cards that already exist? This one is easy. You can always add the minor changes to your outline with additional cards and all you have to do is renumber them once the new cards have been inserted. For example, if you have decided to add a new wrinkle to the actions of a character, simply write that new information on a blue character card and plug it in to its proper place. If you have two minor inserts but don't want to get into a full renumbering of the cards, you can simply add cards 23(a) and 23(b) after card 23 and before card 24.

If you've understood my directions, adding new cards with this type of additional information will not affect the arrangement of the cards. It will only require you to number the cards that contain the new additions. If this is the path you choose to take, add cards, number them accordingly, and get back to writing your script, remaining loyal to your outline.

On the other hand, if during the writing process you suddenly discover that your script would be significantly improved if some major story and/or character information were to change, based on new ideas, you have a huge decision to make because you cannot just add these major ideas into your existing outline without considering the far-reaching ripple effect it will have on your current story line. Decide if the changes are truly important enough to the story to warrant a rewriting and reworking of your outline. If so, you've got your work cut out for you.

If you have this epiphany and it's early enough in the writing process, you need to step away, examine your outline as it currently exists, and make a judgment about whether drastic changes are necessary to write the script with the changes you are envisioning. If the answer is yes, then you need to stop writing and go back to the outlining process. It's permissible to revise the outline if you haven't gotten too far into writing the script, but step away and use the same outlining method.

Let me repeat that. If any little change can be added into your existing outline without causing a problem and affecting the story line, you're in good shape. Just insert another card into the card sequence (23, 23(a), 23(b), 24). But if a drastic change will alter the path of the story significantly and will affect your characters' actions and dialog down the road, and these changes will cause a screenplay-wide jolt that will affect scene upon scene through the original story line, then you need to stop writing and return to the outlining process. There is no getting around this.

You will need to add new cards to address your new thoughts and to replace the cards that no longer fit because they no longer serve your story properly. Once you rearrange them, you need to renumber all the cards. Take some time to double and triple check the changes before you do, because you need to be comfortable with this choice.

STEP 8: You might think I'm crazy, but when I'm writing, I'll use every trick in the book to keep me motivated and on track. For that reason, I always write from the beginning of the outline to the end in the order of the cards, and I never skip ahead or go back. Never. I'm constantly moving forward, never forgetting that I will be going through all of it again during the writing of the second draft.

While you may find it risky or totally nuts, I tear up each card after I've finished addressing it and toss it in the trash, never to return. Every day, as I continue to write, all I need to do is look at the wall to see that I'm making real progress. The cards are vanishing row by row, and that means I'm adding pages to my screenplay and that the outline is doing its job. I know for sure that I'm not leaving anything out, and when the last card is torn up, I will be typing those two wonderful words, THE END.

Now that you're done with your outline and about to start writing, I have to throw in one more warning. If you've truly beaten your outline to a pulp and you remain true to the card outline as it exists on your wall, and it tells the story exactly the way you intend it to, then your script should match your cards when it comes to page count.

However, if your cards show that you expected to reach a certain place in your story by Page 10, but you are already on Page 18 and haven't gotten there yet, then something is wrong. Either it means your outline was way off because you left out a lot of information when creating your cards, or you aren't writing based on your own outline. If I had to guess, I'd say you're not just writing about what's on your cards but you're expanding on the information you thought each card would cover while in the outlining process. In other words, if you thought that a certain yellow action card described a gun fight that would last roughly one minute on screen but your writing of that scene spans three pages, then you've gone beyond the parameters of your outline. Don't panic. Keep moving forward, sticking as closely to your cards as possible, and remember that you can address these issues in your second draft.

BONUS TWO

DEFEATING PROCRASTINATION

I'm not here to learn about screenwriting. One of my instructors at A.S.U. said he took your seminar last time you were in Phoenix, and that you taught people how to deal with the procrastination that keeps them from getting their work done. I don't have a problem with the work itself once I get going, but I do have lots of trouble getting started. I'm really hoping you can help me, because waiting until the last minute has always been my biggest problem when it comes to school. So, when are you going to be talking about that?

Let's do it right now, buddy. I wouldn't want anyone to think I was stalling or subconsciously avoiding the lesson on defeating procrastination. Okay, that was an extremely lame and unfunny joke telegraphed from a thousand miles away. But seriously, the sooner we start, the sooner you and everyone else with the same problem will breathe a big sigh of relief. If you pay close attention for a few minutes and follow some very simple advice, you will leave here convinced that you can work a lot smarter from now on.

Believe it or not, for as insurmountable as procrastination seems to be, it only takes a short time to explain the phenomenon that is plaguing you—and millions of writers everywhere. Once we get through that part of the process, it's easy. So just relax, get comfortable, and rest assured that you'll soon have the tools necessary to take the power away from the procrastination that continually makes you feel guilty or angry at yourself for not being as productive as you know you can be.

I'll start by telling you that I'm a screenwriter, not a mental health professional, and that I have no formal training in psychotherapy, so don't try to sue me for practicing medicine without a license. While I don't have a degree in psychology, what I did have was a long and painful personal relationship with procrastination. I'm happy to announce that we've been divorced since the early 1990s. I was awarded custody of my peace of mind in the settlement and procrastination kept absolutely nothing of mine.

When I was first starting out, I often found myself sitting at my desk for what seemed like hours, doing nothing but looking at the computer monitor. The screen was blank and despite my sincere desire to write, I couldn't bring myself to begin typing. As time passed, all I could do was watch the cursor blink and hate myself more and more for not getting anything done. It got to the point where I began to question whether or not I was even cut out to be a writer or if I had enough real desire to succeed. It was hard to understand what the hell was happening. If I had some talent and opportunities to work as a writer, how could I earn a living if I couldn't put words down on paper? I needed to find an answer, so I sought professional help.

Mind you, I didn't feel like I was going crazy for any other reason, but I was very concerned that I'd never make it as a writer until I could take control of my work habits, or the lack thereof. I was referred to a young lady, fresh from a Master's Program in Counseling, and I spilled my guts out at the beginning of our very first appointment. I had already wasted enough time and wanted the instant cure that same day. That wasn't going to happen, but I want to encourage everyone out there to stay with me on this story because you'll see that it doesn't take years, months, or even weeks to get a grip on procrastination.

My therapist, Tammy, threw all kinds of facts and statistics about procrastination at me. These are important for procrastinators to know.

Procrastination is not a special brand of laziness or even laziness at all. Let's get that straight right now. To me, someone who can do something, but who instead chooses not to do it, might be considered lazy. I never chose to procrastinate, but instead found myself trapped in a pattern of behavior that I couldn't seem to escape. I'm sure that sounds familiar to at least some of you. What we procrastinators have in common is that we all want to achieve at a high level, but don't take the steps necessary to make it happen. We have the drive, but for some unknown reason we just can't get into gear.

Tammy said that procrastination isn't a rare condition. People might not want to admit to it because they think it is a form of mental weakness, but almost everyone procrastinates in some way, at least from time to time. Statistics show that, of those who procrastinate, 40% will not be as productive as they can be, but can still manage to get some work done, while 25% are so stuck in the mud they can't achieve much of anything at all. Studies also show that procrastination typically hits when someone is in their 20s, and begins to dissipate on its own when a person enters their 60s. Who the heck wants to wait that long? Not me.

Before I give you my strategy for how to kill procrastination, I want to make sure you really understand what it's all about so that you can remind yourself of these factors when I'm not in your face talking to you. Also, it will help you even more if you recognize yourself in the description of the character traits and emotional make-up of chronic procrastinators.

For example, it probably doesn't take a lot of convincing for you to believe that students would much prefer to do something fun and easy instead of something boring and difficult. But if you were one of those students who could get away with cramming for exams, or a student able to wait until the last minute to crank out a term paper, or even worse, one of those people who was just clever enough to pass tests without studying very much, then all of the above seemingly positive traits only serve to reinforce bad behavior exhibited by those who never had to work as hard as others. You might be one of those people my Dad referred to as being too smart for their own good.

I guarantee you that if you're a procrastinator who plays mind games with yourself and deliberately lets the time run short when you're under the pressure of a deadline, and claim that you work a lot better "under the gun," then every time you get away with it, you're just reinforcing bad behavior and helping to make procrastination a mightier nemesis in the future.

If intelligence can be linked to procrastination, so can stress and anxiety. I can't speak for anyone else, but I was certainly one of those people who would immediately feel like I was locked in an unpleasant situation when I was forced to accept responsibility for getting some amount of work done, and my first instinct was always to find the escape hatch. Anxiety and high stress levels can be the direct cause of an immediate onset of some very uncomfortable symptoms, from nervousness all the way up the ladder to the feeling of impending doom or death. In some way, if anxiety and stress are attached to your need to complete an assignment, then it makes total sense to want to run away when scary sensations of dread wash over you. Does any of this sound familiar yet? If not, it doesn't mean those factors aren't present in your case. It might just mean that they are buried deep down and that you aren't aware of them.

When I was starting out, I tended to be a perfectionist when it came to my writing. If I was going to have any success at all, I would have to be a lot better than just good at what I do and I didn't see where I had much wiggle room. The constant quest for perfection is already a tough thing to live with all by itself, but when you couple it with being very self-critical, you're in big trouble. You need to attain excellence and if you feel, even for a second, that you are falling short of that standard, you will become your own worst detractor.

While we're at it, let's add two more fun traits to this procrastination cocktail, and you should begin to see how complex this problem really is. Procrastinators are fond of external deadlines set by someone other than themselves. If they had their own way, procrastinators would prefer answering to authority figures who assign tasks and then wait impatiently for their speedy completion. They can't stick to their own deadlines. Also, if you are anything like me, you avoid seeking approval from others because it presents the risk of hurtful rejection. The truth is, if you're going to be a screenwriter, both are things you'll simply need to get over ASAP.

If you're a procrastinator, you probably have a set routine of things you do as you prepare to work. You set the stage but then fail to complete the process because you find a way to actually avoid starting the work itself. You get right to the edge, and then stop. The more you repeat these steps, the more likely it will become a habit that is hard to break. Look at it this way. You have work you need to do, and want to do, such as writing a script, and you keep getting ready to launch into the project, but you continually find a way to stall. You feel as if you are really accomplishing something by getting everything organized and the runway cleared, but all you're doing is postponing the work and the inevitable outcome. Whatever sense of satisfaction you are feeling is coming not from achievement, but merely from the preparation to achieve.

The more you procrastinate, the more depressed you will become. You will chide yourself for not getting on track and you will be harder on yourself than anyone else could ever be. When a friend or family member tells you to start fresh tomorrow, it might give you a temporary boost of energy and improvement in mood because they are giving you permission, the perfect excuse after the fact, for not doing your work. It's a reprieve from the stress you are experiencing as a result of being unproductive. You're off the hook for today, but what about tomorrow and the day after? Anxiety will kick in and when you go to bed, you'll be worried about your inability to work effectively the next day. Chances are, if writing is important to you, you won't get much sleep.

When I was at the peak of my self-destructive procrastination, this is the conversation I would have with myself every night:

"Okay, I'm going to get up early tomorrow, like around 7:00, shower, get dressed, have a quick breakfast, drink my coffee, and then I'm going to spend 10 minutes checking my voice mail. (To keep it real for today, I'll add e-mail to this scenario, even though that distraction didn't exist back then.) If there aren't any legitimate emergencies, I'll be at my desk, ready to work, by 8:00. I'll leave my phone in the other room and I'll write until noon. Then, because I was able to put in four solid hours of work, I will take a one-hour lunch break. I deserve that time off. During lunch, I can check my e-mail and phone messages again, make whatever calls I need to, but under no circumstances will I resume work any later than 1:00 pm. I will work on my script until 5:00 pm, and then I can quit for the day because I've put in eight good hours of writing without distractions. If I feel like it, I can even do another two hours at night, but I don't really need to because I put in a full day, and I'll sleep well knowing I worked hard."

It sounds wonderful, doesn't it? Maybe a little familiar? I'm sure some of you can identify with that inner dialogue, and if you do, then you will also recognize what comes next, because the schedule I laid out for myself never went according to plan. Here's what happened instead:

"Okay, I got up a little late, but only because I had a hard time getting to sleep last night. Hey, I needed the rest and if I had gotten up earlier, I wouldn't have been able to really focus on my writing anyway. To make up for it, I'm not going to shower or get dressed, but I don't need to because I'm working at home today and I don't need to go out, so no one will see me. I'd rather spend my time writing than showering."

Now, instead of continuing to speak for myself, I'll narrate from the perspective of one of the anonymous procrastinators that is certainly in this room.

We, I mean you, left off at getting up a little late, but were about to check e-mail and voice mail and get right to work. Valuable time is wasting. But then, instead of spending a total of 10 minutes on checking your e-mail and voice mail, you sit down at your computer and read the e-mails that are waiting, but then you remember that there are a few e-mails you need to write and that you might as well get them done now while you're already doing e-mail. Then you check your voice mail and even though there are no emergencies, you still feel like there are a few calls you need to make, but they will only take a minute. One of the calls runs long, but you needed to take care of that situation and if you wouldn't have done it now, you wouldn't have been able to focus on writing. Okay, the table is set.

It's time to write, but wait. There was something you wanted to check online and it's related to your script, so technically, it's research. You just forgot to put it in the schedule, but it's important. The internet search turns into reading the news, checking the trades, and checking Facebook and before you know it, it's lunch time. That's fine. You slept late, but you also got a lot done and now that those things are out of the way, there is nothing to do except write. You have a quick lunch, but rather than just eating, you multi-task and check your e-mail one more time and possibly even look to see if anyone from Facebook commented on your post. If you have Instagram, you might want to peek at that too.

Oops! It's late afternoon, and you haven't spent a minute on your script. The day is pretty much blown, but it's all right. You can rearrange your schedule and start now. Sit down at the computer right now at 3:00 pm and begin writing. If you can type until 7:00 pm and then stop for a quick dinner, you will still be able to get a solid four hours of writing in. That's a good way to make up for lost time. Then again, you don't have anything to eat for dinner, so you have a choice to make. You can either run out right now and go to the grocery store for a few minutes, or you can order something to be delivered. It's cheaper if you make something yourself, so you'll just run out quickly and go to the store. Going to the supermarket is actually a good idea because you need some detergent and when you come back, you can put in a load of laundry. That way, while you're busy writing, you can have the washer and dryer running, which will make you twice as productive.

You're about to leave for the market, but realize that you need to get dressed after all. You do it fast without showering, then depart for the store with fingers crossed that you don't run into anyone. You only need to pick up some food and detergent, but hey, since you're here, you might as well get the grocery shopping done now. That will allow you to get even more writing done later because you won't have to spend time another day doing the food shopping. This is working out beautifully! But by the time you get home and make dinner, it's 5:00 pm and you still need to put your meal together.

Meal prepared, you sit down to eat fast. But before you start writing, you load up the washing machine with dirty clothes, and start it up. Wow, this is a bonus. Not only will you be writing tonight, but you're also getting the laundry done. Now, before you get to work on your script, you just want to check your voice mail to see if anyone called. Damn, you have two calls you should probably return and you have a few e-mails to read and need to write a few responses. You're just going to check Facebook for a minute, and then that's definitely it. You're going to start writing and it's only 7:00 pm, which is early. That's great! You can still get at least four hours of writing done tonight. No problem.

But hang on. The washer just stopped and you should put the clothes in the dryer, and some of it needs to be hung up on the shower rod. When you were hanging up the clothes, you noticed that the shower needs to be scrubbed and the mirrors are dirty. You can get that done in 15 minutes, no problem. You'd rather clean it up now than have to do it tomorrow because you don't want to have to stop writing for less important stuff like that. You wipe off the mirrors and scrub the shower but since you're going to clean, you might as well do the toilet, the sink, and the tub. And if you're cleaning the bathroom, you might as well do the other bathroom while you have all the supplies ready. It will save you time later this week.

Okay, it's a little after 8:00 pm, and even though today didn't go as you intended it to, look at all the stuff you were able to get done. You did the grocery shopping, the laundry, cleaned the bathrooms, and those were all things you weren't expecting to do. But it was good for you to do those chores. Sure, you didn't get eight hours of writing done, but you'll do that tomorrow now that all that other stuff has been taken care of. After all, it's crazy to start writing now. If you tried to do four hours now, you wouldn't be done until after midnight and that's just going to make you really tired tomorrow, so you might as well quit for today. You can watch some TV now or play video games, because that will help you to relax so that you can sleep better tonight. And hey, you deserve to take a break. You did a lot today and it can't all be work and no relaxation or recreation. You'll have a beer and watch a few minutes of TV. Then you have a few more beers, and you go to bed at midnight. You feel great because you have a concrete, can't miss plan for the next day. Sure, it's the same plan you had for today, but this time you're going to stick to it.

The next morning, you get up at 7:00 am, according to schedule. You shower, dress, eat, etc. You're at your desk at 8:00 am, all ready to work. But before you start, you just need to check something quick on Facebook because it's your friend's birthday and you'd be a real jerk if you didn't wish him a happy day. While you're there, you see an article that's very interesting so you have to read it, and you see a link to a video on YouTube that's very funny, and then you remember that another friend invited you to dinner next week. Right before you begin to write, you give your friend a quick call to confirm dinner arrangements. You talk for about 15 minutes and you give him an update on your script. You're going to be spending the entire day writing, so you have to hang up. Discipline!

You sit down at your desk and you are just about to begin typing, when you notice that your monitor is really dusty and so is your desk. If you're going to be sitting there all day, it would be better to clean the screen and desk because you don't want to breathe in dust all day. It isn't good for your allergies. You'll wipe this stuff off but if it's this dusty on the desk, you can only imagine how much dust you're breathing in from the carpet. You're just going to vacuum it now. It will only take 10 minutes. You have to think of your health. So, you clean the monitor, desk and carpet and now it's 9:00 am, which means you've already done a few good things for yourself and you're only one hour late in starting to write. That's fine. You can live with that. But you did kind of promise yourself that you would start to take better care of yourself this week, and since you were able to get moving at 7:00 as planned, it wouldn't hurt to take one hour to go for a long walk, maybe three miles, to get into better shape and it will even help you to write because your mind will be clear. The truth is, you do a lot of your best thinking while you're walking and it really isn't good for you to sit at your computer so much, so this will be an excellent use of your time.

While you're walking, a friend calls and asks what you're doing for lunch. You can't go do anything with them because when you're done walking, you have to go back to writing. The friend says he's going to be in your neighborhood and if you like, he can either meet you someplace fast and close by, like Taco Bell, or he can drop something off at your house. Hey, that's a great idea, because if he can drop off your lunch, that will save you even more time. Awesome.

When you get home from your walk, your friend comes by and brings a meal. He says that as long as he's already there, would it be okay if he had lunch with you? Five minutes to wolf down a burrito. No problem. It can't hurt, plus it's stimulating to have some interaction with real people instead of just sitting at your computer all day.

He eats fast, is ready to leave, and then he says he wants to show you a short video on his phone from a mutual friend who is traveling overseas. It's something you'll get a kick out of and it might even inspire you when it comes to your own writing. You watch the clip but that leads to another video, which leads to you wanting to show him a video. Wow, where does the time go? It's already noon and you haven't written a single word.

Sadly, and unexpectedly, that three-mile walk took a lot out of you because you're not in good shape. Not only that, but that heavy Burrito Supreme is making you sleepy. The good news is that it's only noon and this is when you were supposed to have your lunch break, so in a way, you're ahead of schedule because you've already eaten. Maybe you'll feel more energized if you take a nap for an hour? When you wake up at 1:00, it will be the time you were supposed to resume writing anyway, so nothing will be lost. You take the nap, but it appears you were a lot more wiped out than you thought. You unexpectedly sleep an extra hour and get up at 2:00, but that's okay. If you really needed that much rest, it isn't healthy to not listen to your body. You can still get a lot of writing done before dinner. But before you start, you just need to check your e-mails and Facebook for a minute.

Does this silly story resonate with you? I'm sure a lot of it does. And if these examples of things people do instead of writing are different than yours, that doesn't matter. It's the behavior of finding anything else you can think of to do instead of writing that counts. Writers waste days doing this stuff and those days turn into weeks, then months, and the next thing you know, the script isn't any further along than it was half a year ago. Without the right kind of help, the odds of you being able to finish a draft in your lifetime are slim.

Before I give you my tips for murdering your crippling procrastination, I need to give you some background on the two forces that are preventing you from working. Trust me, it's undeniable that one or both of these demons have taken up residence in your head.

The first force is the Fear of Success. Usually, as soon as I mention the Fear of Success as a likely culprit in your procrastination, writers will tell me I couldn't be more wrong. If you want to be a famous writer and make millions of dollars, there is no way you are afraid of success. It's what you fantasize about. It's what you crave.

It doesn't work that way, my friends. The Fear of Success is an incredibly powerful enemy. Chances are you don't even know it's a part of who you are. It's not as if you would ever walk around saying, "I'm afraid of achieving success." It doesn't seem like a fear that makes sense, but it's a beast nonetheless. It will expose its frightening face at the exact moment you are on the brink of achieving some type of goal or accomplishment, or when you are about to make a positive change of some type. As you prepare to cross the threshold to a personal triumph, you suddenly freeze up. You're moving forward and what lay ahead is unknown and therefore something to fear, at least for some people. Others are excited by what they will find around the next corner. Consider this: are you afraid of the past? Most likely not. It already happened. It's over and you survived it, even if some pretty bad stuff occurred back then. But the future can be terrifying.

You say you want to succeed as a screenwriter. If you manage to do so, there are a lot of things that might happen to you, and if you have even an inkling of a Fear of Success, instead of them being fun and rewarding, you seem to perceive them as negative consequences that flow naturally from your success. For example, you may fear these kinds of occurrences:

People in your life will no longer behave the same way toward you, and you will be worried that they aren't being honest with you or that they don't really care about you the way they did before you were successful.

People will want to get money from you, or some other type of help that they don't expect now.

If you're a female writer and you achieve great success, it might severely damage your relationship with the man in your life. He might feel inadequate compared to you and that could be enough for him to leave you before you leave him. There are many cases of wives who went on diets and exercise programs for health reasons and who were able to regain a more youthful appearance which, instead of pleasing their husbands, scared them away. The men worried that their wives might not want to be with them anymore now that the wives looked so good and could catch another man, or because seeing their spouses in great shape made them feel bad about themselves.

Friends or family members may not want anything to do with you because your success reminds them constantly that they are not successful themselves. The disparity between you and them will cause them to not want to be around you, and you might end up alone. It's interesting that some people will come to you for money, while others will avoid you because the trappings of your success make them feel bad about themselves. Any and all of this can be happening subconsciously.

Success as a writer will be achieved by producing a fantastic script. But once you do that, you will have to keep doing it and that's a lot of pressure. If you ever doubted your talent, the necessity of having to keep duplicating your great work will be a lot to live up to. One bad script might sink you.

A Fear of Success will also have you afraid that you will be found out, that your great script was just an accident and that you really aren't a very talented writer after all.

It's amazing to look at these concerns and be confronted with the reality that, while most people celebrate their good fortune and take great pride in their work, those with a Fear of Success do nothing but worry about all the bad things that can happen now that they are about to win the game.

If you're procrastinating because of an unknown, subconscious Fear of Success, there are a lot of things you might do to alleviate the anxiety and stress, but because they are only dealing with the symptoms and not the underlying cause, they will only make things worse.

For example, you can continue to say no to taking on responsibility. You can refuse to let people count on you for anything. You can use your lack of success to hurt people who care for you and are pushing you. You can become extremely stubborn and refuse to do anything until you get a big reward, whether financial or otherwise. You can feel sorry for yourself, and for some writers, being unsuccessful gives you license to be angry and bitter all the time.

Now that I've made all my fellow procrastinators feel like shit, here's the cure for those who suffer from a Fear of Success:

Let's say you want to write a new screenplay. You have an outline, you have the time, and it's time to start. Although you really do want to write, you can't seem to get off the dime. What might you be thinking? "Damn. I have a really good idea and I need to write it because I can't do anything with it until I finish the screenplay, which has to be about 110 pages long. Holy cow, that's a lot of work." If that's the tape that's playing in your head, consciously or subconsciously, I'm not surprised you haven't been able to type FADE IN.

I'll ask you to forget the script for a moment and pretend you want to quit smoking. Researchers say when you've smoked for a long time, it's harder to quit cigarettes than heroin, and that the nicotine addiction is among the most difficult to kick. That's why I'm using this for my analogy. When someone makes the decision to quit smoking, they tend to see it as a monumental obstacle that is almost impossible to overcome. They forget almost immediately that by quitting smoking they have begun a 100% positive endeavor, and that by no longer smoking, they have done something beneficial for their health, their life span, and their general sense of wellbeing.

What happens when you tell a person who wants to quit smoking that he or she can never, ever smoke again? They panic and say, "Wait. Hold on. You mean I can never smoke another cigarette for the rest of my life? That's too long!" Yes, to a smoker, it would seem like an eternity. If you tell a smoker who sincerely wants to quit that they can never, ever smoke again, not even one puff of one cigarette, they won't quit. It will simply be too hard. An impossible feat to accomplish. But the truth is, you don't have to quit smoking forever. No! You only have to refrain from smoking for the next minute. That's all. Do you think you can handle that? Not smoking for a whole 60 seconds? Of course, you can go a minute without smoking. Anyone can. Even a hardcore smoker.

That, procrastinators, is how you kick procrastination's ass.

If you're writing a screenplay, never look at it as if it's a 110 page document. It's too big! Too intimidating! Knowing that you have to write a 110 page script immediately makes you not want to do it. Instead, let's switch to yet another analogy. Think of a salami, one of those extra-long ones that hangs from the ceiling in an Italian deli. Do you know what that salami is? You can choose to look at it as a single object, and since I'm a procrastinator, that's how I see it. It's something too big to eat, if your goal is to eat the whole thing, so why even try? Instead, try visualizing the salami as being comprised of hundreds of thin slices of salami stacked one on top of the other until they add up to that giant salami. Obviously, it hasn't been sliced yet, but use your imagination. That salami can be cut up into hundreds of tiny units that add up to one gargantuan sausage. Isn't that also what your 110 page script is? A long document that is really made up of small increments called pages? Yes, indeed. Small increments are much easier to handle than long documents, and creating them, one at a time, is a lot more manageable than creating a single, very long document. Which would you rather write, one page or 110 pages? I think we can agree on the answer.

Never again look at the script you want to write as being 110 pages in length. That's a daunting task. It will take forever and it can't possibly be fun. Come on, it's too much work. But what happens if you look at your new script as a bunch of small increments that, when added together, total 110 pages? Is it pleasurable to sit at your desk and type 110 pages? Nope. Might it be fun to write just one page? Sure. Can you accomplish a tiny goal like quitting smoking for one minute? Yes. Can you quit forever? Maybe not. See the difference? It's all in the way you look at things, but there is also a method for accomplishing your mission that makes this work.

I have a strategy for outlining screenplays. Once you learn it and you put it into practice, your life as a writer will become a heck of a lot easier. These two processes, outlining and destroying procrastination, go hand in hand. My outlining strategy will also be presented as a part of this class, and trust me, if you allow me to teach you how to do both, you're going to love me and always want to attend my seminars.

From now on, starting this very minute, I want you to think about your script in terms of how many single pages it will take to complete it. Then, to prevent procrastination from creeping into your life, do this. It is mandatory. Are you ready? Set your writing goal at one page per day. That's it. You will be responsible for writing only one page per day. Is that something you think you can handle without too much anxiety and stress? Of course. You know, I swear I just heard a deep sigh of relief coming from a writer in a city that's two thousand miles away.

Let's pretend your outline is already done, and you will stay on pace to write one page per day. Guess what, folks? If that's all you do and you follow a great outline, your very solid first draft will be done in 110 days, which is less than four months. I am willing to bet you money that without using this strategy of having your script based entirely on a foolproof outline and writing it one page at a time, you wouldn't be able to complete a full screenplay that fast. Remember, those three and two-thirds months are going to pass by anyway, whether you write or not. So, why not do it using my method, one page at a time based on your completed outline, and have a great screenplay at the end of that period?

There's one thing about this plan that you have to promise me you will stick to. If you're a master procrastinator, I can tell you what you'll probably do right out of the box. You'll say that you're only going to write one page a day, but in a couple of days, you're going to think it's too easy and you'll write three or four pages that day. You'll feel a sense of accomplishment and you'll believe that you have procrastination licked. And then? You'll get up one day and not feel like writing, so you won't. The excuse you will make for yourself is that you did more than one page a few days back, so you're still ahead. Then, a day or two later you won't do any writing, but that's fine, because you'll just do two pages tomorrow. It won't take very long before that good old anxiety and stress is running your life again because you will have to make up work that you've missed and you will have been knocked totally off course. Suddenly, because you didn't stick with the program, writing will no longer be fun. Don't let it happen. Please. This first time out, strictly abide by my guidelines. No anxiety, no stress, no fear.

If you find yourself doubting me and you're ready to abandon my game plan, answer this: How many times have you started to write a screenplay that you're allegedly excited about, and you haven't finished it in 110 days? How about in a year? How about in 5 years? Do you see a problem here? It's not the story that is preventing you from finishing your script, it's the paralysis that you allow to breed inside your skull. Hell, not only do you plant the seed of fear and doubt in your head, you even fertilize it!

Write one page per day. And when you are done with that one page, do one more thing for me. Reward yourself. Do something insignificant, but enough to make you feel good. When you've completed your page for the day, go to the movies. Buy a song on iTunes. Eat a shrimp cocktail. Make yourself some popcorn and indulge in a silly, guilty pleasure on Netflix. It doesn't have to be anything more than a little pat on the back. Small gestures like that help measure your progress and make a big impact on your mental state. The feeling you get is more important than the value of the object. Give positive reinforcement to the positive act and achievement.

Last thing on this type of procrastination: Forgive yourself for all the time you wasted in the past. Let it go. That was then, this is now. It wasn't your fault, and you know better now. You are free to be infinitely more productive, but only if you buy into the method and don't push it. There is nothing to worry about and your script can't keep you prisoner anymore, unless you want it to.

Now that you understand the Fear of Success and how it gives rise to procrastination in some writers, we need to examine the flip side of the coin, the Fear of Failure.

The Fear of Failure can knock you down and keep you there. I don't know how anyone else feels about it, but it seems like the Fear of Failure makes a lot more sense as something that can be debilitating to a writer than the Fear of Success. Once I explain its characteristics and how it threatens to bog you down, you might want to own this insidious phobia as being a constant in your pursuit of a writing career.

Many writers never finish a screenplay despite the repeated assurances from the tiny voice in their heads that they will do so. They either quit or keep going back over what they have written to fix it or rethink the outline. They will hone it endlessly and hardly ever reach the last page or anything near it. It's the perfect example of the Fear of Failure at work in your life. Quite simply, if you never complete your script, you won't ever have to face judgment on its quality. If you never consider it done and never show it to anyone else, you will never have to find out if you're good enough. That's a beautiful place to hide, behind the excuse that you just haven't had the time or energy to finish. I'm not suggesting that writers do this on purpose, making a conscious decision to avoid the possibility that they will be disappointed. But really, who cares how you end up in this position?

On my first day of kindergarten, I was scared to death of getting off the school bus. I was as sure as I could be that I didn't know as much as the other kids and that I would be humiliated for not being as smart or as ready as everyone else. How deeply was that seed planted in my head? Far enough down that even now, all these years later, I can still feel it. Obviously, I had no choice but to enter the classroom and sit down at my desk. But taking those few steps seemed like walking in heavy, wet cement.

That seed of negativity, that Fear of Failure, was real to me even though it never belonged there in the first place. I was an average kid coming into a strange, new place and meeting new people for the first time. Who wouldn't feel apprehensive at that age? It was natural, but I let it get to me. What I found out later, when I made friends, was that most of the other kids experienced the same fear I did and we all faced it and overcame it, together. If you think back to your childhood and if you remember how you felt in school, or doing things for your parents, you might agree that you learned to have a Fear of Failure at a very early age. It was easy to absorb and it's been with you ever since, in many of your activities, from your college education to playing sports and even to relationships. How many times have you been interested in someone romantically but resisted your instinct and desire to approach them because you were afraid of being shot down? How many times have you not wanted to be given a spot in a competition because you were sure that you would be the person on the team that would be responsible for the potential loss?

When we don't achieve a goal, we are unhappy and maybe even embarrassed, and that shame will hang on like grim death, keeping us scared to try again. It's the same when writing a script. The pages will contain your ideas, the written expression of your talent, plus your hopes and dreams for a good outcome. You are all over those pages, and like I used to tell people when I finished a script, it might as well have been printed with my blood instead of toner. That's how much of myself I poured into my work, and I'm sure many of you feel the same way. If so, then you know how hard it is to hand your screenplay over to someone else to evaluate. If they don't like it, then they can't possibly like you.

One component of the Fear of Failure is the worry that you will make mistakes. What if you do and you don't spot them? Won't that sink your script? Maybe, but use that concern as fuel for the fire. If you don't want your script to contain errors, take whatever steps are necessary to prevent them. Use spell check, but also learn to spell without it. Use Final Draft to format your script, but learn the rules of formatting too. Use all the information available on how to present a script to a reader, and follow those rules. It isn't impossible to become an expert in these things and if you're going to be a writer, you need to master them. The good news is that we learn by making mistakes. It's an old cliché, but it's the truth. If you never made a mistake, you wouldn't have an opportunity to correct it by becoming more knowledgeable. If becoming a more complete writer means you won't make the mistakes you're worried about, then you probably won't repeat them, and that's a huge win.

The truth is, if you don't finish your script, the naysayers win. And by naysayer, I mean other people who are irrelevant, and the part of your brain that has convinced you that you might not be worth a damn as a writer, and that your script is a piece of garbage. Just finish the friggin' thing. Even if it's a horrible first draft, if you make it to the end and you print out a copy that you can hold in your hands, then you can revel in your accomplishment at least for a moment. But you can build on it. Improve it. Make it work for you. That's what professional screenwriters do.

When you finish a script, one that you've worked hard on for a very long time, the next step is to have it read by someone who will dissect it and hopefully give it a passing grade. It's perfectly normal to pace around your living room while you're waiting to hear from the reader, hoping that they like it. But hoping a reader will like your work is exactly what is supposed to happen. You aren't supposed to be so afraid that they won't like it that you never send it or worse, never finish it. That is taking your concern to an unhealthy, unrealistic level.

Knowing this about the Fear of Failure, if you can admit that it all sounds and feels like something you deal with and that it's the source of your trouble, then the solution isn't complicated at all.

The solution to overcoming your lack of productivity is by attacking your Fear of Failure. Do so immediately, and without mercy. You already have an outline you're confident in, so kick its ass. Throw your energy and creativity at it and get it done one page at a time. Let me repeat that. Get it done one page at a time. If you don't let up, before you know it you'll be typing "The End," perhaps for the first time in your career as a writer.

When experiencing the Fear of Success, you might be afraid that you really are a good enough writer to make it but that you will either be exposed as a fraud and ultimately not as good as you think you are, or you might be afraid that you won't be able to duplicate the quality of the script you're working on now, or you might be afraid that the relationships you currently enjoy will somehow be damaged if you achieve success. These doubts keep you from finishing.

With the Fear of Failure, you're worried that you're not good enough from the start, so you don't even try. The only difference between the Fear of Success and the Fear of Failure, at least in my mind, is the starting point. The victim of a Fear of Success thinks they can do it, but then becomes convinced that they're wrong or that reaching their goal will somehow turn out to be destructive. The person suffering with a Fear of Failure never really believes they are capable from the outset.

When attacking your Fear of Failure, follow this basic plan:

1. Accept the fact that writers hear "No" on most occasions. All writers. Rejection is part of the business, so the quicker you learn to expect that it is likely, it won't bother you anywhere near as much. When you realize that most writers, even the A-listers, don't receive perfect scores on everything they write, rejection will lose a lot of its sting. You aren't going to

put all your eggs in one basket, so there is always next time. That's par for the course.

2. Find comfort in the fact that a reader might not like your script, but it isn't a personal insult. They have no reason not to like you as a person and if anything, if you've written something good enough to get to a reader's desk, they will most likely respect you as a professional.

3. Shake things up from time to time and don't allow yourself to become stagnant. Change your methods, rework your schedule, do some things recreationally that will refresh you and recharge your battery. Writing is hard work and you'll need stamina to stay in the fight.

4. If you make mistakes, repair them, and be thankful that you have a chance to learn something new.

5. Don't wait another minute to start writing. You've waited long enough, haven't you? Do it now.

6. Never stop trying. Many writers give up after they failed to hit the jackpot with their first attempt at a screenplay. That's just silly. Please tell me another field of endeavor where a competitor would throw in the towel after their first unsuccessful outing. A boxer who retires after losing his first fight never really had the heart or the commitment to be a boxer. A new teacher who resigns because she was unable to transform every kid in her classroom into an A+ student doesn't have what it takes to be an inspiration to those who want to learn. A writing career is a long-term investment and it isn't an easy path to take. But you can never achieve any measure of success without a consistent effort. Get to work and keep writing!

One last thought on procrastination, and it might be something you need to hear. I often say the Fear of Success is like quicksand, while the Fear of Failure is a prison sentence. They both suck, one way or another. As of now, you don't have to choose either of them or buy a ticket on the procrastination train as you navigate through the turbulent entertainment industry. You have the tools to destroy procrastination before it does any more harm. As soon as you wake up to it, the nightmare will be over.

Oh, yeah. Some writers have won the booby prize and suffer from both the Fear of Success and the Fear of Failure—simultaneously. As you can well imagine, the combination is devastating and the unfortunate souls who are bombarded by both beasts are paralyzed into total inaction. Despite having the talent or aptitude, with these two negative forces battering them at every turn, managing to make any meaningful headway on a script would be nearly impossible. How can I be so sure? You guessed it. I was one of those writers who, until I received my education in all things procrastination from Tammy, was hopelessly incapable of writing. At least I thought I was.

If I could liberate myself from procrastination, write numerous scripts, some very well-received, and have a long career as a screenwriter, so can you. If you recognize the patterns or the worries I've described, please put my game plan into effect as soon as possible. Use my outlining method and apply it to your writing. Recognize your issues for what they are, get out of your own way, and start writing your damn script. But this time, don't just start it, finish it.

INSIDER STORY ONE

THE REWRITE

1996. I was hired to "rewrite" a full length, feature screenplay that needed a little tightening up and polishing. That's all. Nothing too complicated or time consuming. The production company that hired me was under the umbrella of a big movie studio, and all they were waiting on was for me to crank out the newest draft so they could get on the fast track to production.

I was offered "X" amount of dollars to do nothing more than take the amazing first draft and merely clean it up a bit. Straighten out a couple of structural issues, add a joke or two here and there, trim the fat that didn't help to move the story forward, etc. Given the circumstances and the limited amount of rewriting I'd be doing, they didn't feel that I would have a legitimate claim to credit on the project, but they were happy to let the powers that be deal with that issue in the end.

I was given a very nice, fully equipped office overlooking the bend of Sunset Boulevard in Beverly Hills and a copy of the script, plus a deadline. They were anxious for me to be wrapped up in two weeks. It was manageable, and they were of the opinion that it shouldn't take more than that. I grabbed a cup of really good coffee from a place across the street and opened the manila envelope to get a look at this bad boy I needed to attack. All I knew at that point was that it was a comedy.

The packet felt somewhat light and the reason became clear in an instant. The script was only 14 pages long. Not a typo. 14 pages.

Mind you, this was a feature film project and I was expecting to see a completed screenplay in the 105 to 120 page range. Nope. It was 14 pages all in, including the title page.

The first thing I did was to go directly to the head of the production company to ask if they made a mistake and left the rest of the pages on the copier. Nope. Then I asked if this was a practical joke. It wasn't. Apparently, the original writer realized he couldn't finish the work on his own, so rather than attempting to do so, he handed it back to the producers who were then left with the task of finding someone to "rewrite" it.

They came clean and asked if I could just write the whole thing. Uh huh. That's a very different task, folks. I wasn't opposed to taking a script assignment of this nature, but I asked if they actually expected me to do an exponentially bigger job for the same "X" amount of dollars they were paying me to clean up their script just a smidge. Their next words were priceless, but not exactly atypical. "We really don't have a lot of money left in the budget for writing. You see, we already paid the first writer." Well, that's entirely your problem. By the way, one of the producers was an Oscar-winning actor and to see him sit there and help make this argument was pathetic at best. I'd like to see him act in a movie for a few lousy bucks and be told that his salary was so ridiculously low because they already paid another actor who quit the project. I've never won an Academy Award, but I demand the same respect as someone who has.

I turned down the job on the spot. They actually feigned shock. After all, they were giving me this great opportunity. Didn't I know who they were? Yes, motherfuckers, I know exactly who you are. You're the kind of people who derive some kind of twisted pleasure from taking advantage of writers every day of the week. That wasn't going to be me. There's an old adage in Hollywood, that you always get screwed your first time out. This wasn't my first time.

They were desperate, so the negotiations began right there, on the spot, and we soon reached agreement. I would throw away the 14 pages, re-outline the story my own way, and write the entire script from scratch. My fee was then multiplied by a healthy number. We signed a deal memo and they paid me 50% up front that very day. We haggled somewhat on the time frame because they still expected me to be done in two weeks, which was beyond ridiculous. Is it realistic that you can start with a blank screen, no outline, and turn in a solid draft of a screenplay in two weeks? When we came to terms on the deadline, I made my final demand. They had to hire a stenographer, preferably someone who could type 100 words per minute on Final Draft with no errors. If I was going to be working on this monster around the clock, I wanted someone there to take down every word I said, listening intently as I paced a trench in the carpet. They agreed to pay for a Man Friday.

Flash forward to the day I completed the script. I really liked it, thought it lived up to our expectations, and was confident that the producers would share my assessment. I handed it in, and we met the following day to discuss. I, along with the entire production team, sat around a large conference table for a reading and notes. Believe it or not, the big boss said there weren't any. He continued with a couple of sentences I'll never forget. "We could shoot this right now, as is, without a single change. But I have an idea that I think you'll like, so let's go talk." Something was up. The last time I experienced that sensation, a Fleet enema was involved.

In the Executive Producer's office, I was given the good news. The script was fantastic. He loved it. But he figured out a way to take it to the next level and improve it even more. The best part was that it would be super quick. He suggested that I take on a partner for a week or so and that we team up to generate another draft with minor, almost insignificant changes. You see, he had given the script to someone he knew, and that someone had a few novel thoughts on how my script could be made to sing. I told the producer that I would be willing to make some changes, but why bring in another writer? Oh, this wasn't exactly another writer. It was someone with an opinion, but without any actual experience or background as a writer. The last part of the deal was that a rewrite fee would be paid, but I would have to agree to split it equally with this new interloper.

I said no. Absolutely not. If they could shoot the script today as is, which is what the boss said, why go through these unnecessary machinations? The answer was simple. The person with the opinion was the Executive Producer's special friend. How special? Very special. And I was accused of pre-judging this person's abilities without even knowing the first thing about them. Not true. I did know the first thing about them. That's because this special friend hung out at the office every day doing nothing. I had the sneaking suspicion that the EP's special friend would be doing the same thing working with me on the script for half of my fee. Sorry. No friggin' way.

I pointed out that I had completed my end of the bargain when I turned in the script. My contract with the production company had been satisfied. There was nothing more I owed the company. It was time to pay me the rest of what was owed and if they used my screenplay, I could expect to go through the process of determining credit since I basically wrote the entire thing from page one. But alas, I was relying on these folks to do business honorably, the way it should be done, rather than the way some despicable people in Tinseltown prefer to handle things.

As punishment for refusing to work with his special friend, the Executive Producer withheld the second 50% of my fee. He encouraged me to sue him, actually begging me to, so that he could make sure I would spend the first 50% on legal fees. He added that he would now have his special friend rewrite the script alone, so that they could remove my name from the title page. Ha ha! What a mensch.

Now, all these years later, I only tell that story for the benefit of writers who allow themselves to be suckered by producers. Have you been asked to write for free? Have you been asked to make changes on a script without any deal in place? Have you been asked by a producer to let them take your script around town for free to see if anyone is interested? And if they are, the producer would then be your equal partner? I wouldn't be at all surprised. Learn from this situation and don't be victimized.

I never did receive the second 50% of what I was owed under our contract, and the film was never produced. But what did happen is that the Executive Producer who screwed me earned the dubious distinction of being installed as a prominent figure on the WGA's Unfair List, which provides the names of people that writers should never work with. You might think that's karma at work and that the producer got what he deserved, but that's unfortunate and naive. He couldn't give a rat's ass about being on that list. To him, it's like a badge of honor. All it means to him is that he got away with mistreating at least one writer, and he'll do it again if given the chance.

By the way, if you think I'm kidding about the existence of the "Unfair List," check out the following WGA link.

http://www.wga.org/employers/signatories/strike-unfair-list

As with any dealings—Caveat Emptor. I'm doing my best to look after new writers, but the rest is up to you.

INSIDER STORY TWO

WILD PITCH

I've had the pleasure of meeting many writers around the country who yearn for their chance to be on staff at a sitcom or sketch comedy show, and quite a few believe that the work day consists of a bunch of funny men and women who really like each other sitting around, coming up with jokes, and supporting each other's material as if it were their own. That may have been the case on The Dick Van Dyke Show, but that was 1961. Throughout my three decades as a writer/producer, I never seemed to find myself sitting across the table from Morey Amsterdam, Rose Marie or Dick. Several dicks, but never Van Dyke.

Perhaps I was hallucinating every time I was part of a large writing squad, but I don't recall the days and extremely late nights, writing for a comedy series, being a non-stop laugh riot where the staff chuckles, high fives, slaps each other on the back, pounds the table, and cries tears of joy when hearing all the hilarious wit and endless punchlines generated by their buddies. Maybe that's how it is for others, but I don't remember trudging out of my office exhausted after fourteen hours or more on the job, often in the middle of the night, complaining that my ribs hurt from all the hours of belly laughs, thrilled that my friendships with other comedy writers were firmly cemented by all of the mutual appreciation we had for each other's pages.

Yes, I'm being a tad bit of a smartass. I only say all of this, not to be negative, but to give newer writers a more realistic view of the writers' room. It isn't all fun and games, nor should it be. A lot of work needs to get done, and it isn't easy by any means. No matter how talented the staff, there are always things to fix because the star said so, the network said so, the head writer said so, or for one reason or another you can no longer use whatever made its way into the script.

The writing never stops, and to their credit, I never saw a fellow writer say that they had nothing more to give. You do it, even if you are burned out or have run dry. The later it is in the season, the harder it is to come up with anything of quality. At the start of a season, you might have to pitch ideas once a week. That's an under-appreciated luxury. As the episodes roll on, people begin to fizzle out and can no longer think straight, the ideas get weaker and weaker, and instead of giving writers a much-needed break, the head writer will instead do the opposite and schedule more pitch meetings. Now that you've shot your comedy wad and are having trouble conjuring up a good premise, guess what? You'll now need to pitch three times a week. And just when you reach the point where nothing is funny anymore, they start having you pitch every day or multiple times a day. I kid you not.

I was on one show where, near the end of the season, no one had anything left. We were spent. It was miserable. But then, in a stroke of genius and pure compassion, the star of the show let us know that we were lazy, untalented, could all be replaced with a single phone call, and that to help us get motivated he would expect us to pitch three times each day. Oh, and one more thing. No repeat pitches. God forbid you came into the room and presented an idea that you originally submitted earlier in the season. That would be a full-blown disaster.

I was working on a comedy show and it was early in the season. We were on track to do 22 episodes, but later in the cycle a few more were added. It's not that we were pacing ourselves, but the writers were definitely mindful of the fact that we had to come up with literally hundreds and hundreds of pitches, and there was no sense in pitching all of your best stuff early on. Save some of that stuff for when you can't manage a coherent thought, let alone a humorous one. This is something you learn over time, and you can't rely on some other veteran writer on staff to warn you about the reality of the situation. While they may not stab you in the back themselves, many writers won't go out of their way to knock the knife out of someone else's hand either.

It was a Monday and one of the writers on staff, a nice fellow, came into the conference room and when it was his turn to pitch, began his time on the hot seat by announcing that he had been thinking about us a lot over the weekend, that he realized how much he loved all of us, and that he wanted us to know that he could no longer hide his true feelings. His eyes welled up with tears and it was really funny. He had done some acting and this performance was easy for him. Obviously, it was a joke. It was his way of breaking the ice. Most of us laughed. He was such a great guy.

Using a slightly different tact, some writers usually start with a decoy pitch, which is something you would never, ever pitch for real. It would be something so bizarre, you would know it wasn't meant to be taken seriously. Just another kind of laugh getter and tension reliever. I love decoys, the more ridiculous the better. My specialty, on the other hand, is to fake a bail-out on my own pitch, usually by commenting on how bad it is before I even start the pitch itself. It doesn't take long before people begin to anticipate my apologies, which usually puts them in a more receptive mood to hear the pitch.

While most of us at the table enjoyed the pronouncement of affection by this writer, the star of the show who sat at the head of the table was offended. He wasn't the least bit entertained. Instead of letting it go, he let the writer go. Not on the spot, but soon after the meeting ended. In other words, he fired a comedy writer for doing something funny. Wow, what an awesome way to inspire your staff. No one thought he meant it. What was the harm in what that writer did? The star was quick to let us know. The grievous, irreparable harm was that it took precious time away from the business of the show, which was to do mildly amusing stuff on TV. I suppose the people responsible for coming up with the funny stuff for TV were not allowed to do funny stuff in the process. But no one could argue with the star of the show. His word was final.

On that same show just a few weeks later, one of the other writers, also a friendly sort who always pulled his own weight, decided to pitch something with a prop, which was uncommon. I won't tell you exactly what it was, because there are definitely some writers out there who will immediately recognize this story and bust me on who the writer was, who the egomaniacal star was, and what show it was. I don't feel like going through that, so I'll just say this. The fake product was a real product that was doctored up with a fake label. The name of the product poked fun at something dealing with the homosexual lifestyle. He pitched it with a lot of enthusiasm and although it wasn't exactly side-splitting, no one in the room booed or anything like that—except for the star of the show. He took great offense at the pitch. Why, you may ask? He never said, and he didn't have to. The only thing he did say, not unlike Donald Trump in the "Apprentice" boardroom, was "You're fired."

Even though we witnessed this kind of overreaction in the not too distant past, we didn't believe it. Big deal, it was a lame pitch. But you're firing this guy for one errant idea? That was stupid and mean. And yet, the star of the show did it with a smile on his face. The writer didn't believe it was for real, so he continued to laugh and sit there, until the star of the show said, "You heard me. Get your shit and get out." The writer did, and that was the last I saw of him. By the time the meeting was over, his office had been cleaned out and he was gone. It has always been my opinion that the star of the show may have been somewhat homophobic, and hearing anything that referred to homosexuality freaked him the fuck out. Very sad and very, very unrealistic. All I can say is, if you're working in the entertainment industry and you have even the slightest problem with gay people or even the idea of it, then who the hell do you think you're going to work with or talk to? If people from L.A.'s LGBTQ community bug you, you'll have a tough time in Hollywood, and you deserve it.

The two pitching incidents in this story really did happen, on the same show weeks apart, and both were triggered by legitimate comedy writers trying to do something to earn a laugh. They were willing to take risks in pursuit of comedy. To all of the new writers who are dying to get on staff at a funny show, I wish you all the best of luck. I honestly do. I hope you get the job you want. But I also hope you never have to work for an asshole like that one. There are some fabulous fantasies about writing on a TV show. There are also some realities that aren't all that nice. You just need to know that going in.

Despite what I've witnessed and endured, none of it stopped me from working. I hated when it happened, but I chose this profession, so I have to take the good with the horrible. So will you – even though Rob Petrie never did.

INSIDER STORY THREE

BURIED TREASURE

It happened in the 1990s. I was working on a TV show. Late in the season, the head honcho let it be known that he had enough money left in the budget to bring in two more staff writers. They had to exist at the very bottom rung of the ladder, meaning they couldn't demand more than the minimum that he would be offering, plus they might not receive onscreen credit for their contributions.

We were soon told that time was of the essence and that if we knew of anyone who might be appropriate and available, we should let one of the Co-Executive Producers (Co-EPs) know about it right away. After all, they trusted our judgment. I had two people in mind, both of whom could certainly do the job, but this story is about only one of them.

I approached one of the Co-EPs and informed her that I had a friend who would unquestionably be an asset to the show. I gave her a rundown on his credits and talked him up a little. The Co-EP said he sounded like a solid candidate and requested that I have him submit a sample packet. And to streamline the process, it should consist of the kind of material that we were already using on the show.

Back in my office, I called my buddy and encouraged him to send me a sample ASAP. To help him get it done right on the first try, I faxed him some pages from one of our shooting scripts so that he could use our slightly different format as a template. The EP of the show didn't like the standard TV format, so he created his own and we all had to use it regardless of how time consuming it was to manually enter elements that the script software would tell us were incorrect. Yet another example of a boss getting his way on an issue that should never even come up.

My friend faxed me his material and I read it. It was good, but I really wanted him to get the position, so I made some notes and had a quick conversation with him about the changes I was suggesting. He agreed, made the fixes, and faxed it right back. Within a matter of a few hours, this guy was able to send in a very polished sample in our show's silly, mutated format, and his pages seemed very organic to the show. I felt confident about recommending him and I knew that no one else would've been able to get a high-quality packet in faster than he did.

Later that same day, I went back to the Co-EPs office and presented my friend's sample. The Co-EP asked me if I read it and, if so, what I thought of it. I said I had and I thought it was a very strong sample. The Co-EP asked me if I would like to work with this guy, and whether or not he had a personality that would blend well with the team that already existed or would he be a troublemaker. I said that he was all about the work and I didn't know of a single instance in which he made waves on a job. The Co-EP nodded at my answers and then pointed at a tall pile of submission packets that were stacked up on the corner of her desk. They weren't there when I first talked to her that morning.

The Co-EP asked, "Do you see these scripts? The minute we let the word out that we were looking for a couple of writers, every agency in town started to messenger generic samples to the office. Now I have this pile of samples to read, and you know how much that sucks. Instead of doing the work I really need to finish, I'll be reading samples that will most likely suck." I really wasn't all that surprised that agents bombarded the show with samples. That's their job, along with avoiding phone calls. But man, that was quick. I wish my agent moved like that for me.

I assured the Co-EP that my friend's sample was strong, and that it should be read when the opportunity presented itself. I explained that it might actually help to speed up the search and perhaps even save her the brutality of having to pour through hundreds of potentially painful pages.

Here's the move that makes this story stand out in my mind. Instead of interpreting my efforts as being for the good of the show, the Co-EP found another meaning and said, "I'll get to it as soon as I can." The Co-EP then lifted up the mountain of scripts on her desk and slid my friend's submission into a slot near the very bottom. There were probably thirty or forty full scripts ahead of it. I was flabbergasted. What the heck was this about? For a minute, I thought the Co-EP was kidding. Nope. As if it were a logical explanation, the Co-EP said, "I hate it when people recommend their friends, as if they can be objective. Oh, and by the way, I doubt I'll get that far down into the pile. But nice try." The Co-EP went back to work and I walked out of the office, confused and somewhat angry. Mission not accomplished.

I really was objective as hell. My friend put in the work in short order. His sample deserved to be read, and he earned a shot at meeting with the EP. I doubt his sample ever saw daylight again.

In the end, the show did hire a few new writers. One of them was hired over the phone, without a sample, because he was the EP's friend. Believe it or not, the other new writer was hired because he was a friend of the EP's brother. Again, no written sample. He did it by pitching ideas off the top of his head for five minutes. Two other writers were eventually hired for another reason I can't divulge, but it didn't have anything to do with their writing ability. Enough said.

This is the way it is – or the way it can be. Not all the time, but enough of the time that the unpredictable weirdness has to be expected. You have no idea how many occasions I can name where writers were hired with no experience, because they were a producer's cousin. Or hired because they were the son of a network executive whose only previous job was being the son of a network executive, or a Production Assistant who hasn't written anything since a book report in the 10th grade, but who has proven their amazing writing chops by picking up the star's laundry and waiting around all night so they could drop off a script at two in the morning. And while that occurs, writers like my friend spend time and talent writing a great sample that goes right down the elevator shaft because friends apparently can't be objective – even though that same friend was specifically asked to recommend a writer for an open position. That same rule of thumb however, doesn't apply to EPs, whose friends have the inside track to jobs all the time.

My friend didn't have much success with his career, but that Co-EP went on to become the EP on an extremely popular, highly-rated series where a salary of five figures per week or episode is customary. Nice guys finish last, and people who are impossible and downright evil are routinely rewarded for being mean and unprofessional.

Maybe that's just my take on it since I saw the damage being done to an innocent, well-intentioned writer. But it really does happen and it left an impression I won't soon forget. Shit, it's been 30 years since I first started, and although I know better by now, I'm still pissed off.

Oh, yeah. I almost forgot. At a strike meeting in 2007, I ran into that Co-EP. As we passed each other in the crowd, I thought for sure she would recognize me, so I said hello first to be polite. Her reply was definitely in character. "Do I know you?" I replied, "Yes." "Really? What's your name?" "I'm not telling you." And that's how I left it.

ABOUT THE AUTHOR

Jeff Schimmel has been a Writer/Producer since 1986—with his career beginning just before his graduation from law school. Jeff first sold a Cold War spy movie, then collaborated on two screenplays with Rodney Dangerfield and Harold Ramis. Since then, Jeff has worked on highly-rated sitcoms, numerous sketch comedy series and specials, sold a World War Two story to Steven Spielberg, provided script doctoring services, and has written, produced and developed dozens of screenplays and TV projects for ABC, NBC, FOX, HBO, Showtime, Cinemax, Comedy Central, MTV, CMT, Dreamworks, Warner Brothers, 20th Century Fox, MGM/UA, Lionsgate, and many more, plus programs for Canada, Russia, Israel and Bermuda. Jeff has lectured at several prestigious universities and film schools, and since 2010, Jeff has taught his two-day Maximum Screenwriting seminar in cities around the country.

Made in the USA
San Bernardino, CA
27 January 2018